Quick Reference Summary and Documentation Guide

to accompany

The HARPERCOLLINS CONCISE HANDBOOK *for* WRITERS

Peter Dow Adams

Essex Community College

HarperCollins*CollegePublishers*

Quick Reference Summary and Documentation Guide to accompany
Adams: The HarperCollins Concise Handbook for Writers

Copyright © 1994 HarperCollins College Publishers

All rights reserved. Printed in the United States of America. No part of this book may be used or reproduced in any manner whatsoever without written permission, except in the case of brief quotations embodied in critical articles and reviews and testing material for classroom use. For information, address HarperCollins College Publishers, 10 E. 53rd Street, New York NY 10022

ISBN: 0-06-502268-X

94 95 96 97 9 8 7 6 5 4 3 2 1

Contents

Chapter 7
THE PARAGRAPH AS A UNIT OF THOUGHT — 1

Chapter 8
COHERENT PARAGRAPHS — 2

Chapter 9
AVOIDING UNNECESSARY SHIFTS — 3

Chapter 10
SPECIAL PARAGRAPHS — 4

Chapter 11
COORDINATION AND SUBORDINATION — 5

Chapter 12
USING PARALLEL STRUCTURES FOR PARALLEL IDEAS — 9

Chapter 13
AVOIDING MISPLACED MODIFIERS — 10

Chapter 14
ACHIEVING SENTENCE VARIETY — 11

Chapter 15
AVOIDING MIXED AND INCOMPLETE CONSTRUCTIONS — 12

Chapter 16
CHOOSING EFFECTIVE WORDS — 14

Chapter 17
USING APPROPRIATE WORDS   16

Chapter 18
WRITING WITH STYLE   18

Chapter 19
RECOGNIZING PARTS OF SPEECH   19

Chapter 20
RECOGNIZING PARTS OF SENTENCES   24

Chapter 21
FINDING AND REVISING SUBJECT-VERB
AGREEMENT ERRORS   29

Chapter 22
FINDING AND REVISING PRONOUN REFERENCE
ERRORS   34

Chapter 23
FINDING AND REVISING PRONOUN
AGREEMENT ERRORS   35

Chapter 24
FINDING AND REVISING PRONOUN CASE ERRORS   38

Chapter 25
FINDING AND REVISING ERRORS IN VERB FORM   40

Chapter 26
VERB TENSE, VOICE, AND MOOD   43

Chapter 27
VERBALS   46

Chapter 28
FINDING AND REVISING ADJECTIVE AND
ADVERB ERRORS   48

Chapter 29
USING ARTICLES   50

Chapter 31
USING PERIODS, QUESTION MARKS, AND
EXCLAMATION POINTS TO END SENTENCES   55

Chapter 32
AVOIDING FRAGMENTS, FUSED SENTENCES, AND
COMMA SPLICES   56

Chapter 33
USING COMMAS AND SEMICOLONS TO
PUNCTUATE INDEPENDENT CLAUSES   60

Chapter 34
OTHER COMMA RULES   64

Chapter 35
APOSTROPHES   73

Chapter 36
QUOTATION MARKS   78

Chapter 37
OTHER PUNCTUATION MARKS   81

Chapter 38
CAPITALIZATION   86

Chapter 39
ABBREVIATIONS AND ACRONYMS   90

Chapter 40
NUMBERS   93

Chapter 41
ITALICS   94

Chapter 42
HYPHENS   96

Chapter 44
SPELLING   99

Documentation Guide
1 DIFFERENT STYLES OF DOCUMENTATION   D-1
2 MLA STYLE OF DOCUMENTATION   D-3
3 APA STYLE OF DOCUMENTATION   D-14
4 CBE STYLE OF DOCUMENTATION   D-21

Preface

The *Quick Reference Summary and Documentation Guide* to accompany *The HarperCollins Concise Handbook* is divided into two parts. The first part, the Quick Reference Summary, is a brief listing of the rules and definitions presented fully in *The HarperCollins Concise Handbook*. The rules and definitions are presented here in a brief form without explanations and with just brief examples. The second part, the Documentation Guide, contains the information from Part IX of *The HarperCollins Concise Handbook* and is designed to be a fast, easy reference for students writing research papers in the humanities or the sciences. The *Quick Reference Summary and Documentation Guide* may be helpful to you in one or more of the following ways:

- As a quick reference where you can check the details of a rule you generally understand.

- As an expanded table of contents. Browsing through the summary is an easy way to find a particular topic that you need to look up in the text. The right-hand column gives the chapter and section where the rule is discussed in detail.

- As a convenient listing of modes and methods of research, of MLA, APA and CBE documentation, of model entries for Works Cited and Reference lists, and of grammar rules that you can carry with you to the library, the computer lab, or to other places where taking the entire handbook may be inconvenient.

QUICK REFERENCE SUMMARY

CHAPTER 7
THE PARAGRAPH AS A UNIT OF THOUGHT

Rules and Examples	Section
A well-written paragraph should have the following characteristics:	
• *Focus:* a clear topic sentence (which may appear anywhere in the paragraph or may be implied)	7a
• *Unity:* everything in the paragraph helps support the topic sentence	7b
• *Development:* enough discussion, explanation, argument, concrete details, and examples to make the topic sentence both understandable and convincing	7d
The length of a paragraph is flexible in English. Occasionally, it may consist of just one sentence, especially in the case of a transitional paragraph. In general, you should start a new paragraph for the following reasons: • To signal that you are starting a new point • In narration, (see 7e) to indicate a major shift in time • In description, to indicate that you are focusing on a new section or portion of what you are describing • To emphasize a major point by giving it a paragraph of its own • To break up an overly long block of text	7c
One way to develop a paragraph is to organize it using one of several rhetorical patterns: narration, process, description, cause and effect, comparison and contrast, definition, classification, division, and problem and solution.	7e

QUICK REFERENCE SUMMARY

CHAPTER 8
COHERENT PARAGRAPHS

Rules and Examples	Section
Use transitional words and expressions (sparingly) to indicate the relationship between ideas. Transitional words and expressions include *however, therefore, as a result, for example,* and *nevertheless.* It may be stupid to ride without a helmet, but the only person the bare-headed motorcyclist endangers is him- or herself. Therefore, it would seem that this is a case where government has no business interfering.	8a
Repeat key words or phrases or use synonyms that repeat key ideas to ensure that the reader remembers what the key ideas in a paragraph are. My new briefcase is a marvelously well-designed contraption. It is first of all a satchel for carrying papers, but also books, clipboards, tablets, and the like. In addition, this briefcase includes numerous pockets just right for other items. I keep my computer disks in the outer pocket of the bag, sealed shut by velcro.	8b

Be sure to fulfill any expectations you create in your reader.
    There are good arguments on both sides of the controversy surrounding capital punishment.
 	
    (The writer of this sentence has created the expectation that he or she will discuss the arguments on both sides *of this issue. If he or she doesn't, then the reader's expectations will not be fulfilled.)*
	8c

QUICK REFERENCE SUMMARY

CHAPTER 9
AVOIDING UNNECESSARY SHIFTS

Rules and Examples	Section
It is usually confusing to shift from one tense (see 26a–d) to another within a piece of writing. *realized* When I walked into my living room, I ~~realize~~ that my television is missing.	9a
The only time a shift in tense is effective is when it indicates that the time being discussed has changed. I lived in Florida until I was fifteen, but now I consider myself a Californian.	9a
Inconsistency in person or number (see 23a) also confuses the reader. The most common pronoun used inconsistently is *you*. *he or she* When a student decides to register, ~~you~~ should plan to spend an afternoon on campus.	9b
It is effective to shift person and/or number when the meaning requires it. Statistics prove that failing to wear a helmet when riding a motorcycle doubles the risk of motorcyclists' sustaining head injuries and more than doubles the chances that they will require hospitalization from an accident. Therefore, if you are going to ride a motorcycle, you should always wear a helmet.	9b
Once you start with one mood (see 26i), do not shift to a different mood for no apparent reason. Use plenty of concrete examples in your writing and ~~you should~~ focus on one subject.	9c
If you begin a sentence in active voice, do not shift into passive voice for the second half. *she asked me* When my college roommate called me, ~~I was asked~~ for a donation to the alumni fund.	9d
Do not shift arbitrarily between direct and indirect quotation. Mr. Hernandez said that he is firing Jackie because she did not *him* come to work yesterday and she did not call to tell ~~me~~ she was sick.	9e

3

QUICK REFERENCE SUMMARY

CHAPTER 10
SPECIAL PARAGRAPHS

Rules and Examples	Section
Opening paragraphs should accomplish one or more of the following purposes: • Getting the reader's attention • Letting the reader know the point of the essay • Providing background information or context to help the reader "get into" the essay itself	10a
The opening paragraph is sometimes best written after you finish a draft of the entire paper. If you choose to write it first, revise it carefully after you finish the first draft.	10a
The closing paragraph serves primarily to let readers know that they have reached the end of the paper. In it you can use one of the following techniques: • Restate the thesis • Emphasize the action you want the reader to take • Refer to an event or image from the opening • Use a question or quotation	10b
The closing paragraph is often quite brief.	10b
Transitional paragraphs alert the reader to a major shift from one section of your paper to another.	10c
In writing dialogue, use a new paragraph each time the speaker changes.	10d

QUICK REFERENCE SUMMARY

CHAPTER 11
COORDINATION AND SUBORDINATION

Rules and Examples	Section
Use coordination to avoid a series of short simple sentences and to indicate the relationship between ideas. *and* *but* I washed the dishes ⌿, ∧Hector made a salad ⌿, ∧Shoko read the paper.	11a
Use coordination to join only ideas that are logically equivalent. *who* Jerri, ∧is parking her car, ~~and she~~ lives in Boise.	11a
Use the coordinate conjunction that indicates the logical relationship between ideas. *so* We had no money, ~~and~~ we stayed home all weekend.	11a
Place the main idea of a sentence in the main clause and not in a subordinate clause. *While* ∧Helene was reading her history textbook, ~~when~~ a loud explosion rocked her apartment.	11b
Use the subordinating conjunction that best expresses the meaning you intend. *Because* ~~Although~~ we had no insurance, we were not reimbursed for our losses in the fire.	11b
Avoid using *in which* unless the noun it modifies is something a person can be *in*. *for* He has a job at Blue Cross and Blue Shield ~~in~~ which he is paid $9.25 per hour.	11b
Avoid excessive coordination or subordination. I opened the door and ⌿ saw Mr. Salinas ⌿. ~~and~~ I asked him to *H* come in and look at my television ⌿. ~~and~~ ∦e said it was a model that had a lot of problems.	11b

Rules and Examples	Section
The relative pronouns *who, which,* and *that* may be used as subjects of clauses. The man who smokes a cigar is the detective.	11c
Relative pronouns may be used as direct objects. The butterfly pin that Margot will wear to the barbecue is very pretty.	11c
Relative pronouns may be used as objects of prepositions. Paco, from whom I received a letter, was my host in Spain.	11c
Relative pronouns may be used as possessives. The woman whose car I hit is taking me to court.	11c
In an adjective clause, the relative pronoun and *be* verb may be omitted if the following conditions are met: • The adjective clause is restrictive. ***Correct*** The man who is wearing a blue hat is angry. ***Correct*** The man wearing a blue hat is angry. ***Correct*** Stefan Martin, who is wearing a blue hat, is angry. ***Incorrect*** Stefan Martin, wearing a blue hat, is angry. • The *be* verb is in the present tense. ***Correct*** The woman who was wearing a blue hat was angry. ***Incorrect*** The woman wearing a blue hat was angry. *(This sentence is incorrect if it is intended that the woman was wearing the hat—in the past.)* • The *be* verb is followed by a participle or a prepositional phrase. ***Correct*** The women wearing blue hats are angry.	11c

Rules and Examples	Section
Correct The woman in the pool is my sister. **Incorrect** The woman angry is my sister. *(The relative pronoun and be verb may not be omitted if the verb is followed by an adjective such as angry.)* • The relative pronoun is the subject of the adjective clause. **Correct** The woman on the phone is my sister. **Incorrect** The woman I speaking to was my sister. *(The relative pronoun is not the subject here but the object of the preposition to.)*	11c

Adverbial clauses can precede or follow independent clauses.
 	
    Adverb clause   *Independent clause*
Because his dog had died, Larry did not enjoy the party.
 	
    Independent clause   *Adverb clause*
Larry did not enjoy the party because his dog had died.
	11d

One type of noun clause is derived from questions that ask for information.
  Why she ever dated Jim is a mystery to me.
 	
This type of noun clause can be introduced by one of the following words:
 	
  what   where   who
  whatever   wherever   whom
  when   which   whose
  whenever   whichever   why
	11e

A second type of noun clause is derived from questions that can be answered with *yes* or *no*. This kind of noun clause is introduced by the words *if* or *whether*. My daughter asked if she could go to the movies. I wonder whether the presidential candidates will debate in my hometown.	11e

Rules and Examples	Section
The third type of noun clause is always introduced by *that*. That she was embarrassed was clear by the color of her face. We decided that Leonie will go to Eastern Europe.	11e
When noun clauses beginning with *that* are used as direct objects, *that* can always be omitted. ***Correct*** I am happy that you are coming to dinner. ***Correct*** I am happy you are coming to dinner. When noun clauses beginning with *that* are used as subjects, *that* cannot be omitted. ***Correct*** That you are coming to dinner is a great surprise. ***Incorrect*** You are coming to dinner is a great surprise.	11e

QUICK REFERENCE SUMMARY

CHAPTER 12
USING PARALLEL STRUCTURES FOR PARALLEL IDEAS

Rules and Examples	Section
Items joined by a coordinate conjunction must be parallel. *playing* I enjoy swimming and ~~to play~~ tennis.	12b

Items in a series must be parallel.
    Maxine remembered to finish her economics paper, walk her
 	
    balance
dog, and ~~balancing~~ her checkbook.
	12c

Items compared using *than* or *as* must be parallel. *do* I would rather cook dinner than ~~doing~~ dishes.	12d

Items in an outline or list must be parallel.
    We need to rent the following:
 	
  • three Macintosh computers
  • one printer
  • ~~reserve~~ a suite of rooms at the Hilton.
	12e

Repetition of a word or two at the beginning of each item in a series is not advisable unless such repetition seems to make the sentence clearer.
    The instructor and I talked about the final exam, which I will
 	
    about
have to miss, ^my reasons for needing to take an incomplete in
 	
    about
the course, and ^my plans for next semester.
	12f

QUICK REFERENCE SUMMARY

CHAPTER 13
AVOIDING MISPLACED MODIFIERS

Rules and Examples	Section
Place modifiers in sentences so that it is clear which word they are modifying. I read about the accident that my brother had in the paper.	13a
A limiting modifier, such as *almost* or *only*, should be placed in front of the verb only when it actually modifies the verb. If it modifies another word in the sentence, it must be placed in front of that word. Greg only slept for four hours last night.	13b

Dangling modifiers occur when a phrase at the beginning of the sentence is not followed by the noun or pronoun it modifies. Correct dangling modifiers by placing the noun or pronoun the phrase modifies immediately after the modifier or by rewriting the phrase so that it is a clause with its own subject.
 	
             I let the spaghetti sauce boil over.
Cooking dinner last night, ~~the spaghetti sauce boiled over~~.
 	
While I was
  ∧cooking dinner last night, the spaghetti sauce boiled over.
	13c

A modifier is said to be "squinting" when it is placed in a sentence in such a way that it could be modifying either of two different words. Correct a squinting modifier by moving it to a position where there is no confusion about the word it modifies. The baby-sitter told us quietly to go upstairs and look at the baby.	13d
A *split infinitive* occurs when a modifier appears between the word *to* and the verb that follows it in an infinitive. Split infinitives that cause awkwardness should always be revised; those that do not result in awkwardness should, nevertheless, be revised if there is any chance that your audience will find them problematic. Paula hoped to soon open a French bakery.	13e

10

QUICK REFERENCE SUMMARY

CHAPTER 14
ACHIEVING SENTENCE VARIETY

Rules	Section
When you are revising, watch for a lack of variety in sentence length. In particular, avoid long sequences of short sentences. Do not merely replace a sequence of short sentences with a sequence of compound sentences. Instead, combine them into more complex sentences that indicate the relative importance of ideas. If a paragraph consists of medium to long sentences, however, it *is* a good idea to place an important idea in a short sentence for emphasis.	14a
Use sentence openers, including transitional expressions, various phrases, and adverb clauses, to achieve sentence variety.	14b
Use inverted word order to create sentence variety, but use it sparingly. Begin sentences with *there* or *it* only when you have a strong reason for doing so.	14c
Use commands, questions, and quotations to provide variety in sentence structure.	14d

QUICK REFERENCE SUMMARY

CHAPTER 15
AVOIDING MIXED AND INCOMPLETE CONSTRUCTIONS

Rules and Examples	Section
Mixed constructions occur when a sentence starts out with one kind of grammatical structure and changes to a different one somewhere in the middle. Mixed constructions should be revised. Because Ray did not attend the first class, ~~so~~ he has never understood the point of the course.	15a
Mixed meaning, or *faulty predication,* occurs when the subject and the verb are mismatched—when they don't make sense together. Revise the sentence to eliminate the awkwardness. Be especially careful with sentences that include the patterns *something is when, something is where,* and *the reason is because.* One reason not to use chemical pesticides on your lawn is *that* ~~because~~ they can make your pets sick.	15b
Delete pronouns that merely repeat the meaning of the noun subject of the sentence. The answer to your question / ~~it~~ is right in front of your nose.	15c
Be careful to use *in which* only to modify nouns that you can put something "in." My job, ~~in~~ which I have had for two years, does not offer me much security.	15d
Do not omit words in elliptical constructions if doing so makes the meaning unclear. *of* Houng was afraid ∧ and mad at his landlord. *my* My husband and ∧ accountant will be arriving at seven.	15e
State comparisons fully enough so that no ambiguity is created. *she liked* My mother always liked me more than ∧ my sister.	15e
When comparing an item with all others in the same class, use the word *other.* *other* The ginkgo tree is older than any ∧ tree that still exists.	15e

Rules and Examples	Section
In English, you may omit the subject only if the sentence is imperative—if it gives a command (see 19c). *it* If a country uses raw materials from another country, ∧has to pay for them.	15e
Whenever you place your subject after a linking verb (see 19c), you must put either *there* or *it* in front of the verb to make the sentence complete. *There are* ~~Are~~ a large number of books about the Vietnam War.	15e

QUICK REFERENCE SUMMARY

CHAPTER 16
CHOOSING EFFECTIVE WORDS

Rules and Examples	Section
Avoid confusing two words that sound alike but have different meanings and spellings. *too* It is ~~to~~ hot to play tennis today.	16a
Avoid using words that do not exist in Standard English. *a lot* We picked ~~alot~~ of tomatoes.	16a
Avoid errors that result from using unfamiliar words. *profane* I object to ~~profuse~~ language on television.	16a
Avoid misusing ordinary words. *I hope* ~~Hopefully,~~ the bus will be here in five minutes.	16a
Be especially careful to use the appropriate preposition. *on* It's all right to develop a dependence ~~for~~ dictionaries.	16b
Avoid *unfortunate chimes*, the use of the same word twice in a single sentence, particularly if its meaning is different in the two instances. *almost* Tara argued for ~~about~~ three hours about the rights of animals.	16c
Eliminate words that contribute nothing to the effectiveness of the sentence. *blue* Helene bought a ∧dress. ~~that was blue in color.~~	16d
Use intensifiers—words like *very, extremely,* and *exceedingly*—sparingly. Nelson was ~~extremely~~ tired after an hour of basketball.	16d
Avoid redundant expressions—saying the same thing twice. As Bruce entered ~~into~~ the army, he realized he had made a terrible mistake.	16d

Rules and Examples	Section
Avoid awkward expressions. The ~~outcome of the~~ reorganization will bring greater productivity.	16e
Avoid *prefab phrases*—expressions that have been used over and over, particularly if they have been used in television commercials. The professor rescheduled his final exam. ~~for our convenience.~~	16f
Avoid excessive humility. ω ~~It is only my opinion, but I think w~~e should cancel the meeting.	16g
Be aware of the connotation of words as well as their denotations. *childlike* He has a ~~childish~~ attitude toward life.	16h
Have reference books handy when you are writing.	16i
Use the power of your computer, especially the "search" or "find" function, to help you edit for word choice errors.	16j

QUICK REFERENCE SUMMARY

**CHAPTER 17
USING APPROPRIATE WORDS**

Rules and Examples	Section
Avoid the use of *sexist expressions*, that is, expressions that make assumptions about people based on their gender or that assume that being male is "normal" for human beings or that all human beings are male. *Human beings are* s ~~Man is a~~ tool-using animal ^. *Doctors* *their* ~~A doctor~~ must understand ~~his~~ patients' fears.	17a
Use jargon with great care. When you are writing for a general audience, use it sparingly and explain each technical term. When you are writing for other professionals in your field, you should still be careful not to overuse jargon. **Excessive Jargon:** The makers and comakers of this note hereby . . . agree that the holder's right of recourse against them . . . shall not be affected by extending the time of payment without their assent. . . .	17b
Avoid using language that is pretentious, language that is sometimes called *bureaucratese*. *The weekly staff meetings are intended to improve communication.* ~~The aim of the periodic management staff interfacing sessions is to maximize communication.~~	17c
Use slang only when it serves a specific rhetorical purpose. Do not allow it to intrude inappropriately into an otherwise formal text. I hope that you will consider my application for the position you have advertised. ~~since I am hard up for a job.~~	17d
Avoid using obscenity and profanity in your writing unless you are certain they won't offend your audience or when you either intend to offend or don't care if you do. *care* I don't ~~give a damn about~~ what the manual says we should do.	17e

16

Rules and Examples	Section
Use metaphors and similes to enliven your writing. *Metaphors* and *similes* are figures of speech that help readers understand a concept by comparing it with something they are likely to be familiar with. A simile makes the comparison by using *like* or *as*. A metaphor states that one thing *is* something else. **Metaphor** She felt that merely to go so far away from home was a kind of death in itself . . . (Eudora Welty) **Simile** They sat immobile on their antique bench like a row of crusty oysters. (John Barth)	17f
Avoid using *mixed metaphors:* two metaphors for the same idea in the same sentence. Like a sailboat pushed by a strong wind, the bill sailed through Congress. ~~under a full head of steam.~~	17f
Avoid *clichés:* expressions that are worn out from overuse. C ~~Beyond a shadow of a doubt,~~ clichés will make your writing seem unimaginative.	17g
Do not use archaic or obsolete language unless you intend to sound old-fashioned for a particular rhetorical purpose. *soon* I will talk with you ~~anon~~ about your disappointment.	17h

QUICK REFERENCE SUMMARY

CHAPTER 18
WRITING WITH STYLE

Rules and Examples	Section
In general, use concrete and specific words instead of abstract and general ones. *green plastic basket of blueberries* I took a ~~container of fruit~~ out of the refrigerator and dumped it on the counter.	18a
Select concrete words that support the focus of your writing. In a paragraph in which you intend to describe cleaning strawberries, sentence 1 would be more focused than sentence 2: 1. I took the little green plastic basket of strawberries out of the refrigerator and dumped them on the counter. 2. I took the package of strawberries out of the almond toned G.E. refrigerator, which we had purchased just a few months earlier, and dumped them on the beige Formica counter.	18a
Select telling details—words that really capture the essence of what you are describing. Example 1 includes more telling details than example 2: 1. Most of them were perfect—a deep red with little greenish seeds all over them. A few had light green tips. 2. Most of them were perfect—red and plump and delicious. A few were less ripe.	18a
As you write, weave back and forth between the abstract and general and the concrete and specific. *Abstract and general* This chauvinism may have been a reaction to the constant racial prejudice we encountered on all sides. The neighborhood cops were always running us off the streets and calling us "dirty greasers," and most of our teachers frankly regarded us as totally inferior. (Hank Lopez) *Concrete and specific*	18a
Choose strong verbs. *ripped open slapped* Stephen ~~opened~~ the package and ~~placed~~ the bandage on my leg.	18b

QUICK REFERENCE SUMMARY

CHAPTER 19
RECOGNIZING PARTS OF SPEECH

Rules and Examples	Section
Nouns	
Nouns are words that stand for persons, places, or things. *teacher, boy, island, city, test, ocean, apple, plate, table, kitchen*	19a
Nouns can be *names* of persons, places, or things. *Mr. McGregor, Joseph Stalin, Florida, Seoul, Kleenex, Titanic*	19a
Nouns can stand for things that are concepts or ideas as well as concrete things. *truth, confusion, problem*	19a
Nouns usually can take *a*, *an*, or *the* in front of them. *a banana, an orange, the guava*	19a
Pronouns	
A *pronoun* can stand for a particular person such as the speaker, the person spoken to, or a person spoken about. 　　　　　　　　　　　　　*her* My older sister asked me to give ~~my older sister~~ a ride.	19b
A pronoun can stand for an unknown or unspecified person or thing. Someone sent me a scary note.	19b
The noun a pronoun stands for is known as its *antecedent*. My older sister asked me to give her a ride.	19b
Pronouns can be classified into seven basic types:	
Personal pronouns stand for particular people or things: *I, you, he, she, it, we, they, me, him, her, us, them.* I gave him my best necktie.	19b
Possessive pronouns indicate ownership: *my, your, yours, his, her, hers, its, our, ours, their, theirs.* My brother can never remember his Social Security number.	19b

Rules and Examples	Section
Reflexive pronouns stand for someone who or something that is the receiver of the same action for which he, she, or it is also the doer: *myself, yourself, himself, herself, itself, ourselves, yourselves, themselves.* Roxanne should not blame herself for what happened.	19b
Intensive pronouns take the same forms as reflexive pronouns but are used to emphasize a noun or another pronoun. The teacher himself broke the overhead projector.	19b
Relative pronouns introduce dependent clauses: *who, whom, whose, which, that, whoever, whomever, whichever, whatever.* The woman who chaired the meeting did not recognize me.	19b
Interrogative pronouns are used to ask questions: *who, whom, whose, what, which.* What did she mean by that remark?	19b
Demonstrative pronouns identify or point out specific persons, places, or things: *this, that, these, those.* This is the best soup I've ever eaten.	19b
Indefinite pronouns stand for unknown or unspecified persons, places, or things. Everyone is invited to the party.	19b
Pronouns change their form depending on how they are used in sentences. The woman who gave me a ride is crazy. The woman to whom I gave a ride is crazy.	19b
Verbs	
A verb can express an action, something someone or something *is doing, was doing,* or *will be doing.* Marco runs every morning for an hour. Marco ran every morning for an hour. Marco will run every morning for an hour.	19c
Words that are normally nouns can be verbs if they express something someone is doing. Joanie roped a bull in thirteen seconds.	19c
Verbs can also link the subject with something that comes after the verb. My mother was a cabdriver for three years.	19c

Rules and Examples	Section
Verbs can be helping verbs, which appear in front of main verbs. Norm **is** thinking about joining the navy.	19c
To + a verb is always a verbal (an infinitive) and is never the verb in a sentence. Vince wanted **to buy** a new motorcycle. (*The verb in this sentence is* wanted.)	19c

A verb + *ing* is the verb in a sentence only if it is preceded by a helping verb; otherwise, it is a verbal (either a gerund or a participle), not a verb.
 	
      No helping verb
Joining the navy is not so easy these days.
    Verbal
 	
          No helping verb
Lance remembered **looking** into the window.
Verbal
 	
Lance was **sleeping** when I called.
Helping verb   Verb
	19c

Adjectives	
Adjectives are words that modify (describe, identify, or quantify) a noun or pronoun. A **green** sweater lay on the bed.	19d
Adjectives can be located in front of or following the words they modify, or they can follow a linking verb. The **small** kitten opened his eyes. The student, **angry** about her grade, walked into the dean's office. She is **happy** about the meeting.	19d
Other parts of speech, such as pronouns, verbals, and nouns, can be used as adjectives. **His** hat blew off in the storm. (possessive pronoun) The **crying** baby is my little sister. (verbal, or more precisely, a participle) I got a **car** phone for Christmas. (noun)	19d

Rules and Examples	Section
Adverbs	

Adverbs are words that modify verbs, adjectives, other adverbs, prepositional phrases, clauses, and whole sentences.
 	
Bruce walked slowly into the bank.
     —Verb
 	
The restaurant is quite near the bank.
        —Prep. phrase
 	
The extremely tall woman sat down.
Adjective
 	
My knees often ache, especially when it rains.
Dependent clause
 	
She spoke very quietly.
     —Adverb
 	
Undoubtedly, it will rain tomorrow.
       —Sentence
	19e

Adverbs often but not always end in *-ly*. **-ly Adverbs** *beautifully, extremely, sadly, slowly, suddenly, softly* **Adverbs without *-ly*** *almost, fast, very*	19e
Not and *never* are always adverbs. We did not hear the phone. We never get home before seven o'clock.	19e

Rules and Examples	Section
Prepositions	
Prepositions are words that introduce prepositional phrases. We looked in the basement. She is the mother of the bride. My dog ran after the bus.	19f
Prepositional phrases begin with a preposition, end with a noun or pronoun, and may have adjectives in between. Preposition Adjectives Noun ↓ ↓ ↓ in the small box	19f
Conjunctions	
Conjunctions are words that connect words, phrases, or clauses. Mike or Liz will pick you up at the airport. Jake looked in the desk and on the counter. Jeff opened the door, and Mr. Li walked in.	19g
Coordinating conjunctions join items that are grammatically equal. Marissa and Lisa are giving a party.	19g
Correlative conjunctions work in pairs to join items that are grammatically equal. Neither the teacher nor the students noticed the man lurking in the hall.	19g
Subordinating conjunctions join dependent clauses to the rest of the sentence. The woman who lost her collie was very upset.	19g
Interjections	
Interjections are words that express surprise or strong emotion. Oh! What have you done to my cat?	19h

QUICK REFERENCE SUMMARY

CHAPTER 20
RECOGNIZING PARTS OF SENTENCES

Rules and Examples	Section
The simple verb of a sentence consists of the main verb and any helping verbs. Mr. Ochoa should have left me a note.	20a

A *transitive verb* is an action verb used with a word that is the receiver of the action.
          Transitive   Receiver of
          verb   the action
  Nachelle broke her glasses.
	20a

An *intransitive verb* is also an action verb, but it appears in sentences with no word that is the receiver of the action.
         Intransitive   Does not
         verb   receive the action
  Ms. Tan slept at my house last night.
	20a

When transitive verbs are in active voice, the subject is the *doer* of the verb, and the *receiver* of the action of the verb appears following the verb. When verbs are in passive voice, the subject of the sentence is the *receiver* of the action of the verb, and the *doer* of the verb appears in a prepositional phrase beginning with *by*, or doesn't appear at all. **Active Voice** Einstein discovered relativity. **Passive Voice** Relativity was discovered by Einstein. **Passive Voice** My favorite cup was broken.	20a
When two or more main verbs appear in the same sentence, they are known as a *compound verb*. The doctor opened the door and walked into the office.	20a

The *subject* of a sentence is the person or thing *doing* the verb. The subject is most often a noun or pronoun, but can also be a verbal or a clause.
 	
         ┌──── Noun
  Freud discovered the existence of the unconscious.
	20b

Rules and Examples	Section
Pronoun They left on the six o'clock bus.	20a
Verbal Smoking can cause lung cancer. *Clause* Whoever found my watch did not try to return it.	
The subject usually precedes the verb, but in questions and sentences beginning with *there* or a prepositional phrase, the subject may follow all or part of the verb. (In the following example, subjects are underlined once; verbs are underlined twice.) Did your father send you any money? Whom was Maggie arguing with on the phone? There were three reasons for his mistake. There is something rotten in the state of Denmark. In the closet was a large basket of pears.	20b
The subject cannot be part of a prepositional phrase. The color of her eyes was hazel. (Color *is the subject of the sentence, not* eyes, *which is part of the prepositional phrase* of her eyes.)	20b
In imperative sentences, the subject is *you understood*. (You) Bring a dollar to the meeting on Saturday. (The subject of this sentence is understood to be *you*.)	20b
A sentence can have a compound subject, that is, more than one subject. Mushrooms and onions are good in a salad.	20b
A *direct object* is a noun or pronoun that stands for who or what receives the action of the verb. The ball struck a telephone pole.	20c

An *indirect object* is a noun or pronoun that stands for the person who or the thing that is receiving the direct object.
              Indirect   Direct
              object   object
Stew gave   Amy   a   necklace   for her birthday.
	20c

Rules and Examples	Section

Prepositional phrases start with a preposition and end with a noun or pronoun; in between, one or more adjectives may modify the noun.
   We placed the dishes in the sink.
   We put the leftovers in the new frost-free refrigerator.
	20d

The noun or pronoun at the end of a prepositional phrase is known as the *object of the preposition*.
                              Object of
                              preposition
   Hank mailed a donation to the   Red Cross.
	20d

A *subject complement* is a noun or pronoun that comes after a linking verb and is being equated with the subject, or an adjective that comes after a linking verb and modifies the subject.
   Charlotte's mother is a fire fighter.
   The teacher was proud of us.
	20e

An *appositive* is a noun that, together with its modifiers, follows another noun and stands for the same person or thing as the first noun. My teacher, a country music fan, is taking some of us to the Randy Travis concert this weekend.	20f
A *parenthetical expression* is a word or phrase that is not essential to the meaning of a sentence but adds extra information, a fact, an example, a comment, or a digression. Nathaniel Hawthorne is, according to most literary scholars, a major American novelist.	20g
An *absolute phrase* consists of a noun or pronoun and a participle (not a verb) together with any modifiers or objects of the participle. His nose bleeding profusely, the young camper ran into the house.	20h
An *independent clause* must have a subject and a verb and express a complete thought; it cannot "leave you hanging" or expecting more. **Independent Clause** Bells ring. **Independent Clause** The small yellow bird with black wings is a goldfinch.	20i

Rules and Examples	Section
Independent Clause After he learned to read, Frederick Douglass began to plan his escape. **Not Independent Clause** The small yellow bird with black wings. (no verb) **Not Independent Clause** Began to plan his escape. (no subject) **Not Independent Clause** After he had learned to read. (incomplete—leaves you hanging)	20i
Incompleteness caused by the use of pronouns does not prevent a group of words from being an independent clause. **Independent Clause** She left it on the front porch.	20i
Groups of words that include verbals but no verbs can easily be mistaken for independent clauses. **Not Independent Clause** The car speeding around the curve in the highway. (Speeding *is a verbal, not a verb*.) **Not Independent Clause** A corkscrew to open the wine with. (*To open is a verbal, not a verb*.)	20i
A sentence can contain more than one independent clause. I wanted to order chocolate cake for dessert, but I am on a diet, so I just ordered coffee.	20i
A *dependent clause* is a group of words that contains a subject and a verb but is unable to stand as a sentence by itself because it feels incomplete or leaves you hanging. I rolled over and went back to sleep when my alarm went off. The woman who made the speech used to live on my block.	20j
A dependent clause used to modify a noun or pronoun in a sentence is called an *adjective clause*. The car that Maurice bought was a real lemon.	20j

Rules and Examples	Section
A dependent clause that modifies the verb, an adjective, or an adverb in a sentence is called an *adverb clause*. When it started to rain, the children ran into the garage.	20j
A dependent clause used for any function usually filled by a noun is called a *noun clause*. Whoever called me at midnight last night has a warped sense of humor.	20j

**QUICK REFERENCE SUMMARY
CHAPTER 21
FINDING AND REVISING SUBJECT-VERB
AGREEMENT ERRORS**

Rules and Examples	Section

The basic rule for subject-verb agreement in the present tense is as follows:
• If the subject is singular, the verb must have an -s ending.
    barks
  One dog ~~bark~~ every morning.
• If the subject is plural, the verb does *not* have an -s ending.
  Two dogs bark~~s~~ every morning.
	21a

Be especially careful to check subject-verb agreement when verbs end in the sounds -*sk* or -*st*.
    wastes
  This car ~~waste~~ too much gasoline.
	21b

I and *you* are treated the same as *plural* subjects; that is, the verb does *not* have an -s ending.
  I leave~~s~~ early every Friday.
  You leave~~s~~ early every Friday.
	21c

The rule for subject-verb agreement with the verb *be* is as follows:
• If the subject is the pronoun *I*, use the form *am*.
  I am tired of feeling helpless.
• If the subject is singular and not *I*, use the form *is*.
  She is tired of feeling helpless.
• If the subject is plural or the pronoun *you*, use the form *are*.
  Students are tired of feeling helpless.
  You are tired of feeling helpless.
	21d

When *be, do,* or *have* is used as a helping verb, only the first helping verb changes to agree with the subject; the main verb does not change, nor do any helping verbs other than the first one.
  My Macintosh is being~~s~~ repaired.
  My Macintosh and my IBM are being repaired~~s~~.
	21e

Rules and Examples	Section
Use *is* with singular subjects other than *I* and *you*. Use *am* with *I*. Use *are* with plural subjects and *you*. *is* *are* My sister ~~are~~ a dancer. My sisters ~~is~~ dancers. *am* *are* I ~~are~~ a dancer. You ~~is~~ a dancer.	21e
Use *do* as a helping verb with plural subjects; use *does* with singular subjects. *does* Laura Charles's column ~~do~~ make me angry. Laura Charles's columns ~~does~~ make me angry.	21e

Use *have* as a helping verb with plural subjects; use *has* with singular subjects.
 	
   has
My father ~~have~~ built a garage.
 	
   have
My parents ~~has~~ built a garage.
	21e

For all *helping* verbs other than *be*, *do*, and *have*, do not change the form of the verb to agree with the subject. (See also 19c) Rochelle should~~s~~ buy that ring. Rochelle and Julie should buy that ring.	21e
Generally, verbs do *not* change their forms to indicate subject-verb agreement in past or future tenses. One dog barked~~s~~ last week. One dog will~~s~~ bark tomorrow morning.	21f

The verb *be* in the past tense takes the form *was* with singular subjects and *were* with plural subjects.
 	
    was
One bird ~~were~~ singing when I awoke.
 	
    were
Two birds ~~was~~ singing when I awoke.
	21f

Rules and Examples	Section

The subject will never be part of a prepositional phrase, so don't accidentally make your verb agree with the object of a preposition rather than the subject.
 	
            Prepositional
            phrase   *has*
The cause of these incidents ~~have~~ not been discovered
(The subject of the sentence is cause, which is singular.)
	21g

Nouns in phrases that begin with *as well as, in addition to, together with, accompanied by,* and *along with* are not part of the subjects of sentences. *is* My father, together with his dog, ~~are~~ more than I can bear for a weekend.	21g
If subjects are joined by *and,* they are generally plural. *are* Cardinals and kingfishers ~~is~~ my favorite birds.	21h
Singular subjects joined by *or* are singular. *s* Langston or Reggie drive me to work every Friday.	21h
Plural subjects joined by *or* are plural. *are* Raisins or bananas ~~is~~ good in Cream of Wheat.	21h

If a singular and a plural subject are joined by *or,* the verb agrees with the nearer subject.
 	
             has
The students or the teacher ~~have~~ to apologize.
 	
            have
The teacher or the students ~~has~~ to apologize.
	21h

For purposes of subject-verb agreement, indefinite pronouns fall into three groups: • Most are singular *(another, each, either, anybody, anyone, anything, everybody, everyone, everything, nobody, no one, nothing, somebody, someone, something.)* *was* Each of the glasses ~~were~~ broken.	21i

Rules and Examples	Section
• A few are plural (*both, few, many, several, two* or any larger number.) 　　　　　*were* 　Both of the examples ~~was~~ confusing. • A third group can be singular or plural depending on the noun at the end of the prepositional phrase that follows the pronoun (*all, any, more, most, much, none, some, half* or any other fraction, *some*) 　　　　*were* 　Some of the tomatoes ~~was~~ rotten. 　　　　*was* 　Some of the milk ~~were~~ spoiled.	21i
A *collective noun* stands for a group of people. 　*army, audience, band, class, committee, couple, crowd, family, group, jury, team,* and *troop.* Collective nouns are usually treated as singular subjects because, even though they represent a collection of people or things, that collection is being considered as a unit. 　　　*wants* 　The class ~~want~~ to take the final exam on Friday. Collective nouns are treated as plural subjects when the members of the group are being considered as individuals. 　　*are* 　The committee ~~is~~ not able to agree on a meeting time.	21j
The number is always singular; *a number* is always plural. 　　　　　　　　*is* 　The number of students who drop out of school ~~are~~ too large. 　　*are* 　A number of students ~~is~~ planning to quit school this spring.	21j
In sentences that begin with *there,* the subject usually follows the verb. 　*are* 　There ~~is~~ three cups of coffee left.	21k

Rules and Examples	Section
In sentences beginning with a prepositional phrase, the subject *may* follow the verb (but often it appears in its normal location). Under that bed live~~s~~ four of the cutest kittens in the Western Hemisphere. Under that bed, four of the cutest kittens in the Western *were* Hemisphere ~~was~~ born.	21k
In sentences with linking verbs, the verb must agree with the subject and not the complement. *is* My favorite dessert ~~are~~ strawberries and cream.	21l

A relative pronoun (*who, which,* or *that*) is either singular or plural depending on its antecedent.
     is
A student who ~~are~~ late for class should enter the room quietly.
     are
Students who ~~is~~ late for class should enter the room quietly.
	21m

The relative pronoun is the expression *one of those ____ is* generally plural.
     are
She is one of those women who ~~is~~ always on time.
The relative pronoun in the expression *the only one of those ____* is generally singular.
     is
She is the only one of those women who ~~are~~ always on time.
	21m

Words that are plural in form but singular in meaning require singular verbs. *is* Measles ~~are~~ not a disease to be taken lightly.	21n

QUICK REFERENCE SUMMARY

CHAPTER 22
FINDING AND REVISING PRONOUN REFERENCE ERRORS

Rules and Examples	Section
When you use a pronoun, make sure that only one word can be interpreted as its antecedent. *the Girl Scout* Nancy bought some cookies from the Girl Scout, and then ~~she~~ walked across the street.	22a
Avoid using pronouns like *this, which,* or *it* to refer vaguely to some large idea. *the revision* My committee decided to revise the bylaws, but ~~it~~ took us about a month.	22b
A pronoun must refer to a specific noun or pronoun; it may not refer to an antecedent that is merely implied by the verb, by an adjective, or by a possessive noun. *their artwork* When the children finished painting, we hung ~~them~~ on the refrigerator.	22c
Pronouns should not be placed so far away from their antecedents that the reader has difficulty figuring out what the antecedent is. The professor used to be a taxicab driver in New York City, who teaches my favorite class.	22d

QUICK REFERENCE SUMMARY
CHAPTER 23
FINDING AND REVISING
PRONOUN AGREEMENT ERRORS

Rules and Examples	Section

The general principle of pronoun agreement is that a pronoun must agree with its antecedent
• In number
              his
   A man should not smoke ~~their~~ pipe in an elevator.
• In person
              their
   People should try to avoid accumulating large debt on ~~your~~ credit cards.
• In gender
              her
   A woman should be able to tell a secret to ~~his~~ brother.
	23a

When pronouns do not agree in number, writers have three options:
• Change the pronoun to a singular form.
           his or her
   Each of the drivers started ~~their~~ motor at the same time.
• Change the antecedent to a plural form.
    T   *s*
   ~~Each of~~ ʈhe drivers started their motor∧ at the same time.
• Recast the sentence so no pronoun is needed.
  The drivers' motors started at the same time.
   ~~Each of the drivers started their motor at the same time.~~
	23a

Writers should avoid using the masculine pronoun *he* to refer to antecedents that do not specify gender and may, in fact, include women as well as men. *his or her* Someone had left ~~his~~ notebook in the classroom.	23b

When a pronoun refers to two antecedents joined by a conjunction,
• If the conjunction is *and,* the antecedent is always plural.
              their
   Marcia and her sisters liked to talk about ~~her~~ childhoods.
	23c

Rules and Examples	Section
• If the conjunction is *or* or *nor* and joins singular antecedents, the antecedent is singular. *her* Marcia or Sandy left ~~their~~ notebook in my car. • If the conjunction is *or* or *nor* and joins plural antecedents, the antecedent is plural. *they are* Blueberries or strawberries are delicious on cereal when ~~it is~~ in season. • If the conjunction is *or* or *nor* and joins a plural and a singular antecedent, the pronoun should agree with the nearer antecedent. *their* Either Peter or his parents will loan you ~~his~~ car for the weekend.	23c
When a pronoun has an indefinite pronoun as an antecedent, you must determine first whether that indefinite pronoun is • Always singular (see chart below) *his or her* Everyone should turn ~~their~~ first draft in on Friday.	23d

Indefinite Pronoun Number

Always Singular	Always Plural	Sometimes Singular, Sometimes Plural
another	both	all
each	few	any
either	many	more
every	several	most
neither	two or any number	much
one	greater than two	none
every ⎤	⎡ thing	some
any ⎥ +	⎢ one	half or any other fraction
no ⎥	⎣ body	
some ⎦		

The bracketing at the bottom of the left-hand column provides a way of remembering twelve different pronouns: *everything, everyone, everybody, anything, anyone, anybody, nothing, no one,* and *nobody,* all of which are always singular.

Rules and Examples	Section
• Always plural (see chart on page 36) *their* Both of my brothers have lost ~~his~~ wallets. • Singular or plural depending on the noun in the prepositional phrase that follows the indefinite pronoun (see chart on page 36) Some of the effort that Rosalind put into her paper would have *it* been more fruitful if ~~they~~ had been devoted to proofreading.	23d
Collective nouns as antecedents are usually treated as a unified group. Therefore, they are considered singular. *its* The jury has decided on ~~their~~ verdict.	23e
Only when the group members are being considered as individuals are collective nouns treated as plural antecedents. *themselves* The jury argued among ~~itself~~ until three in the morning.	23e

QUICK REFERENCE SUMMARY

CHAPTER 24
FINDING AND REVISING PRONOUN CASE ERRORS

Rules and Examples	Section
The *subjective case* of pronouns is used for the following: • Pronouns that are subjects of sentences 　She called Theresa this morning. • Pronouns that are subjects of clauses within sentences 　The woman who called Theresa was my mother. • Pronouns that are complements 　It was she who called you last night.	24a
The *objective case* is used for the following: • Pronouns that are direct objects 　Theresa called her yesterday. • Pronouns that are indirect objects 　Theresa had sent her a book about yoga. • Pronouns that are objects of prepositions 　Theresa sent the book to her as a belated birthday present.	24a
Complements, which are in subjective case, follow linking verbs. 　It was he who caused all the confusion.	24b
Direct and indirect objects, which require objective case, follow action verbs. 　Mr. Ortega sent me a book, so I thanked him.	24b
Pronouns in compound constructions must still follow the rules for case with subjects and objects. 　Maggie and I explained our objections to Carl and her.	24c
To determine case in a sentence with a compound construction, sometimes it helps to separate it into two sentences. Once you have determined the correct form of the pronoun, return the sentence to its compound form. 　Kelly and I opened the package.　　Mark had delivered it to Kelly and me. 　　Kelly opened the package.　　Mark had delivered it to Kelly. 　　I opened the package.　　Mark had delivered it to me. 　　(I *is the correct form.*)　　(Me *is the correct form.*)	24c

Rules and Examples	Section
Pronouns used as appositives should be in the same case as the nouns or pronouns they are in apposition to. 　The winners, she and Craig, each received one thousand dollars. 　The checks will be sent to the winners, Craig and her, within the next thirty days.	24d
When *we* or *us* is used before a noun, use the form that agrees with the case of that noun. 　We students are not being treated fairly. 　This school should pay more attention to us students.	24e
To determine case in comparisons with *than* or *as*, mentally fill in the *understood* phrase and the correct form of the pronoun will be clear. 　My mother likes my sister better than [she likes] me. 　My mother likes my sister better than I [like my sister].	24f
Who is the subjective form; *whom* is the objective. To determine which form is correct, identify the clause in which the *who* or *whom* appears and put it in natural word order (subject-verb-object). In this way, you can determine whether the *who* or *whom* is a subject or an object and put it in the correct form. 　I know the man who hired you. 　　who hired you 　I know the man whom you hired. 　　you hired whom	24g
Normally, use the possessive case for pronouns (and nouns) that modify gerunds. 　His singing did not impress the judges.	24h
If the emphasis is on the person represented by the pronoun rather than on the action represented by the gerund, then it is correct to use the objective case before a gerund. 　The judges did not hear him singing.	24h

QUICK REFERENCE SUMMARY

CHAPTER 25
FINDING AND REVISING ERRORS IN VERB FORM

Rules and Examples	Section
Regular Verb Forms	
Verbs in English have five forms: **Base form** base form Most people talk while they eat dinner. **Past tense** base form + -ed (-d) We never talked during breakfast in my family. **Past participle** base form + ed (-d) If we had talked, no one would have answered. **Present participle** base form (minus silent e) + -ing Once my mother was talking to herself. **-s form** base form + -s (or -es) Now she talks at breakfast all the time.	25a

Many verbs have irregular forms of the present tense, the past participle, or the present participle. If you are not sure of the correct form, check it in a dictionary.
 	
      went
 Luis ~~goed~~ to the store an hour ago.
 	
      eaten
 Helena has ~~ate~~ lunch already.
	25b

Phrasal verbs are two- and three-word combinations that include a verb and one or two *particles* (a preposition or an adverb).
     boil over   call off   have on   pick up on   shut off
     blow up   check out   leave out   put on   take back
     break down   hang up   look down on   run out of   walk out on
	25c

Intransitive phrasal verbs cannot be separated. She was slow to catch to the game on	25c

Rules and Examples	Section
Some transitive phrasal verbs can be separated or together, some must be separated, and some must be together in a sentence. Unfortunately, there is no rule for determining which need to be separated and which can be together. The only way to be sure is to check the chart in 25c or an ESL dictionary.	25c

Lie is transitive and means "to recline or rest on a horizontal surface"; you cannot *do* it to someone or something.
 	
  lie
Usually, I ~~lay~~ down on the couch to watch television.
 	
  lay
Last night I ~~laid~~ down for an hour after dinner.
 	
  lain
After I have ~~laid~~ there for a few minutes, I often fall asleep.
 	
Lay is transitive and means "to place something or someone in a horizontal position." Of the two verbs, *lay* is the one you can *do* to something else like a towel.
 	
  lays
The newspaper deliverer ~~lies~~ the paper carefully on our front porch.
 	
  laid
Yesterday she ~~lied~~ it on the sidewalk.
 	
  laid
After she has ~~lain~~ it down, she puts a brick on top of it.
	25d

Include -s endings on regular verbs when the subject is third-person singular; leave -s endings off when the subject is not third-person singular. *s* Mr. Thomas unlock˄ the door to his store every morning at eight. His clerks arrives̸ at about nine o'clock.	25e

Include -ed endings on regular verbs in the past tense; be especially careful to add them to verbs for which the -ed is hard to pronounce.
 	
  d
They are suppose˄ to be there by eight-thirty.
 	
  ed
Last week, Mr. Thomas ask˄ them to try to be more punctual.
	25f

Rules and Examples	Section

Linking verbs and helping verbs may not be omitted in Standard Written English.
 	
    is
Mr. Thomas ∧ very understanding, but he needs to be a little more strict.
 	
    has
He ∧ been too easy on his workers.
	25g

Be may not be used in place of *are, am,* or *is* in Standard Written English.
 	
    are
They ~~be~~ taking advantage of his easygoing nature.
 	
    is
I think he ~~be~~ getting a little tougher with them.
	25g

QUICK REFERENCE SUMMARY

CHAPTER 26
VERB TENSE, VOICE, AND MOOD

Form	Formation	Use	Section
Tenses			
Present tense	Base form	Describes events happening at the time of writing	26a
		Describes a habitual or regularly occurring action	
		States general truths or scientific facts	
		Describes actions of literary or artistic characters	
		Describes future events for which there is a fixed time	
Past tense	-ed ending	Describes events that took place in the past and do not extend into the present	26a
Future tense	will + base form	Describes events that take place in the future	26a
		Describes events that are predictable	
Past perfect	had + past participle	When two events in the past are discussed, use past perfect for the earlier one.	26b
Present perfect	has or have + past participle	Describes events that started in the past and are either completed before the present or continuing up to the present	26c
Future perfect	will have + past participle	When two events in the future are discussed, use future perfect for the earlier one	26d
Progressive Aspects			
Present progressive	are, is, or am + present participle	Describes an action in progress at present	26e

Form	Formation	Use	Section
Past progressive	*was* or *were* + present participle	Describes an action in progress in the past	26e
Future progressive	*will be* + present participle	Describes an action in progress in the future	26e
Present perfect progressive	*has* or *have been* + present participle	Describes an action in progress in the past and up to the present	26e
Past perfect progressive	*had been* + present participle	Describes an action in progress up to a certain time in the past	26e
Future perfect progressive	*will have been* + present participle	Describes an action in progress up to a certain time in the future	26e
Voice			
Active voice	Subject is performer of action of the verb; direct object is receiver of the action.	All situations except those listed under passive voice below	26g
Passive voice	Subject is receiver of action of the verb; performer of the action of the verb, if present, is in a prepositional phrase beginning with *by*.	Performer is unknown. Writer wishes to conceal identity of performer. Writer wishes to emphasize the action. Writer wishes to emphasize the receiver of action.	26g
Subjunctive Mood			
Subjunctive present tense	Base form without *-s* ending or *be*	*If* clauses that are contrary to fact. *As though* and *as if* clauses. *That* clauses following verbs that express a demand, a request, a requirement, or a suggestion	26i

Form	Formation	Use	Section
Subjunctive past tense	Past tense form or *were* (never *was*)	*If* clauses that are contrary to fact *As though* and *as if* clauses *That* clauses following verbs that express a demand, a request, a requirement, or a suggestion	26i

The following chart illustrates the formation of various tenses, moods, and voices for one regular and one irregular verb. The form for a singular subject, where it differs from the plural form, is given in parentheses.

Form	walk	be
Indicative Mood		
Regular present tense	*walk* (walks)	*are* (is, am)
Regular past tense	*walked*	*were* (was)
Regular future tense	*will walk*	*will be*
Regular past perfect	*had walked*	*had been*
Regular present perfect	*have walked* (has walked)	*have been* (has been)
Regular future perfect	*will have walked*	*will have been*
Progressive present tense	*are walking* (is walking)	*are being* (is being)
Progressive past tense	*were walking* (was walking)	*were being* (was being)
Progressive future tense	*will be walking*	none
Progressive present perfect	*have been walking* (has been walking)	none
Progressive past perfect	*had been walking*	none
Progressive future perfect	*will be walking*	none
Subjunctive Mood		
Regular present tense	*walk* (never walks)	*be*
Regular past tense	*walked*	*were*
All others are same as indicative.		

QUICK REFERENCE SUMMARY

CHAPTER 27
VERBALS

Rules and Examples	Section
Infinitives and gerunds can both function as subjects, subject complements, appositives, adjective modifiers, objects of prepositions, and objects of verbs.	27a
While gerunds and infinitives can both function as subjects of a sentence, it is more common to use gerunds as subjects. Eating spaghetti is fun.	27a
While gerunds and infinitives can also both function as appositives, it is more common to use gerunds as appositives. The next step, writing the conclusion, is easy.	27a

Both infinitives and gerunds can be used to modify adjectives. When the infinitive is used to modify an adjective, the meaning suggests future time. When the gerund is used, however, it indicates something that is a general truth or happening at a particular time. Gerunds can be used only following the adjectives *hard, worthwhile, easy,* or *difficult.*
   It is hard drinking hot coffee.
   I am happy to lend her a hand.
	27a

Gerunds and infinitives can both function as objects of verbs. Some verbs can be followed only by a gerund; some can be followed only by an infinitive. Many verbs can be followed by either a gerund or an infinitive.
   They enjoy going to movies.
   She wants to eat ice cream.
   He stopped buying a newspaper.
   He stopped to buy a newspaper.
	27a

Infinitives tend to show purpose or something that is related to the future (i.e., something potential or hypothetical). Gerunds, on the other hand, are more general, more descriptive, less active, and show something that is real, true, fulfilled, or experienced.
   Maria hopes to paint the garage on Saturday.
   Maria enjoys reading in a quiet place.
	27a

Rules and Examples	Section
Present participles are formed by adding -*ing* to the present-tense form of the regular verb. Past participles are formed by adding -*ed* or -*en* to the present-tense form of the verb. **Present participle** *walking, taking* **Past participle** *walked, taken*	27b

Participles are used to form tenses.
   Mr. Johnson was talking on the phone to the president.
   He has talked to the president many times.
	27b

Participles are also used as adjectives in sentences.
   We had an exciting day at the casino.
   My parents were exhausted at the end of the day.
	27b

QUICK REFERENCE SUMMARY
CHAPTER 28
FINDING AND REVISING ADJECTIVE AND ADVERB ERRORS

Rules and Examples	Section
Adjectives modify **Nouns** — contemporary novelist **Pronouns** — it was very interesting	28a
Adverbs modify **Verbs** — nervously gives a speech **Adjectives** — exceedingly cruel **Other Adverbs** — very carefully	28a
Use the adverb form to modify verbs, adjectives, and other adverbs. *quickly* He answered too ~~quick~~ and was sorry afterward.	28a

After linking verbs, use an adjective, not an adverb. Linking verbs include all forms of the verb *be* and the following, known as *sensory verbs: appears, feels, looks, seems, sounds, smells,* and *tastes.*
 	
      sad
Ms. Linkwood looked ~~sadly~~ when she heard the news.
 	
However, sensory verbs can also be used as action verbs.
 	
      sadly
Ms. Linkwood looked ~~sad~~ at her dead cat.
	28b

Comparative adjectives and adverbs are formed by adding an *-er* ending to shorter words or by using the word *more* in front of longer words.
    tall   taller
    beautiful   more beautiful
	28c

Rules and Examples	Section

Superlative adjectives and adverbs are formed by adding an *-est* ending to shorter words or by using the word *most* in front of longer words.
   tall   tallest
   beautiful   most beautiful
	28c

Use comparative forms when comparing two things or people.
              easier
   Of the two books, this is the ~~easiest.~~
	28c

Use superlative forms when comparing more than two things or people.
       fastest
   she is the ~~faster~~ runner of the ten women in her class.
	28c

Don't use both the *-er* ending and the word *more* or the *-est* ending and the word *most* with the same word. She was ~~more~~ smarter than her sister.	28c

In formal writing, don't use comparative or superlative forms with modifiers that are absolute.
      nearly
   She is the most ∧ perfect athlete in her class.
	28c

Don't use double negatives unless you intend the positive meaning that results from the two negatives canceling each other out.
      anything
   I don't remember ~~nothing~~ about last night.
	28d

When a series of modifiers comes before a noun, the modifiers should be placed in the following order. (There is actually more flexibility about the order than this chart indicates; however, this order will generally be correct.)

Order of Adjectives

Article or Demonstrative, Possessive, or Indefinite Pronoun	Numbers	Quality or Characteristic	Size or Shape	Color	Other Noun	Noun
a	one	expensive	large	green	bamboo	chair
the	six	impressive	small	red	picture	frame
this	first	noisy	round	black	dining room	table
those	third	elaborate	wide		automobile	tire
his		simple			felt	hat
José's		new				
some						
many						

QUICK REFERENCE SUMMARY

**CHAPTER 29
USING ARTICLES**

Rules and Examples	Section
If you are using *a* or *an,* use *a* before words beginning with a consonant sound; use *an* before words beginning with a vowel sound. 　*a* uniform　　　　*an* hour 　*a* one dollar bill　*an* L-shaped room	29a
Determiners are a category of words that precede nouns and modify the meaning of those nouns. Only one determiner can be used for each noun. **Articles**　　**Other Determiners** a, an　　　any　　this　　your　　my　　possessive the　　　　each　　that　　our　　his　　nouns 　　　　　　either　these　their　her 　　　　　　enough those　　　　its 　　　　　　every 　　　　　　neither 　　　　　　no 　　　　　　some	29b
Singular proper nouns do not take the articles *a* or *an.* 　Central Park　　　　　Alaska-Canada Highway 　Notre Dame　　　　　Indiana State University	29c
In general, singular proper nouns do *not* take the definite article *the.* 　Charles Street　　　　Lansing Community College 　Mount Fuji　　　　　　Doctor Hernandez 　Lake Superior　　　　New York City 　Louise White　　　　　Oregon 　Boston　　　　　　　Pennsylvania Avenue	29c
In general, plural proper nouns take the definite article *the.* 　the Williams　　　　　the Rocky Mountains 　the Kims　　　　　　the Great Lakes	29c

Rules and Examples	Section
Geographic terms, colleges and universities, empires and dynasties, museums and libraries, buildings, organizations, religions, and languages are frequently exceptions to the three basic rules for using articles with proper nouns. See 29c.	29c

Common nouns can be classified according to the following four criteria:
   Countable or Uncountable   *marbles* versus *milk*
   Singular or Plural   *one book* versus *six books*
   Definite or Indefinite   *that car* versus *a car*
   Definite or Generic   *those automobiles* versus *automobiles*
	29d

Always use an article with singular countable nouns *a* Tomorrow he is going to look at ˄ used car. *An automobile* ~~Automobile~~ is an expensive thing.	29e

Use the article *a* or *an* with singular countable nouns that are not definite—that are not specifically known to the writer and reader.
         a
Mr. Tan has to buy ˄ car this weekend, so he can drive to work on Monday.
 	
        a
He realizes that ˄ car is almost a necessity in American society.
	29e

Use the article *the* with singular nouns that are definite—that are specifically known to the reader and writer. *The building* ~~Building~~ where he works is not located near a bus line. *the* He also cannot afford to move from ˄ apartment where he lives because it is very inexpensive.	29e
Use the article *the* with definite plural nouns. *the* He looked at ˄ cars that Jan had recommended.	29e
Use the determiner *some* with indefinite plural nouns. *some* There must be ˄ cars for sale for under five thousand dollars.	29e

Rules and Examples	Section
Do not use an article with generic plural nouns. *Car* ~~The car~~ dealers expect customers to bargain with them. Mr. Tan knows that ~~the~~ car advertisements must be read carefully.	29e
Use the article *the* with definite uncountable nouns. *the* Mr. Tan was aware of ∧ reputation of car dealers for driving hard bargains.	29e
Use no article with generic uncountable nouns. The dealer assured Mr. Tan that ~~the~~ nervousness is a normal reaction.	29e
Exceptions to the basic rules for articles with common nouns include the following: diseases, body parts, appliances, trains and buses, destinations, and words in a series.	29e

On the following pages you will find two charts that provide a visual summary of the conventions for using articles with nouns in English.

Selecting Articles for Proper Nouns

Does the proper noun belong to one of these groups: geographic terms, names of colleges or universities, buildings, empires, organizations or religions?

No.

Is the noun singular or plural?

- Singular. → **Use no article.**
- Plural. → **Use the.**

Yes.

Which group does the noun belong to?

- Geographic terms, organizations, or religions.
- College or university.
- Empire or dynasty. → **Use the.**
- Building. → **Use the.**

Geographic terms, organizations, or religions.

Is the noun the name of a nation, organization, or religion that includes a word that would be a common noun if it were not part of the name?

- Yes. → **Use the.**
- No. → **Does the noun stand for an organization or religion?**
  - Yes. → **Use no article.**
  - No. → **Does the noun stand for a region, desert, peninsula, ocean, gulf, river or canal?**
    - Yes. → **Use the.**
    - No. → **Use no article.**

College or university.

Is the noun of the form (city or state) (State) University or College?

- Yes. → **Use no article.**
- No. → **Is the noun of the form University of (city or state)?**
  - Yes. → **Use the.**
  - No. → **Consult a dictionary.**

Selecting Articles with Common Names

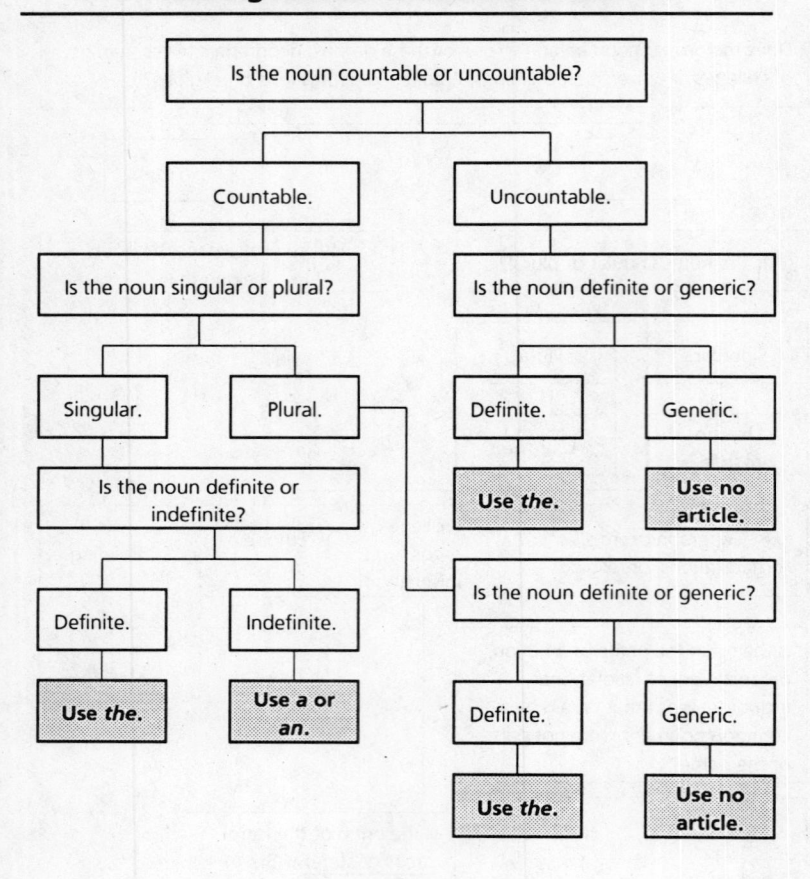

```
Is the noun countable or uncountable?
├── Countable.
│   └── Is the noun singular or plural?
│       ├── Singular.
│       │   └── Is the noun definite or indefinite?
│       │       ├── Definite. → Use the.
│       │       └── Indefinite. → Use a or an.
│       └── Plural.
│           └── Is the noun definite or generic?
│               ├── Definite. → Use the.
│               └── Generic. → Use no article.
└── Uncountable.
    └── Is the noun definite or generic?
        ├── Definite. → Use the.
        └── Generic. → Use no article.
```

QUICK REFERENCE SUMMARY
CHAPTER 31
USING PERIODS, QUESTION MARKS, AND EXCLAMATION POINTS TO END SENTENCES

Rules and Examples	Section
Use a period to end a sentence that makes a statement. Helena opened a bank account.	31a
Use a question mark to end a sentence that asks a question. Did you remember to bring your wallet?	31a
Use an exclamation point to end a sentence that expresses strong emotion. In formal writing, use exclamation points sparingly, if at all. Michael is a fool!	31a
Use a period, not a question mark, at the end of an indirect question. Next he asked if I was hungry.	31b
Use question marks to separate a series of questions, even if they are not complete sentences. The use of capital letters to begin each question is optional (see 38g). Should I say yes? Say no? Run away?	31b
When a sentence that makes a statement ends with a quotation that is a question, place the final question mark inside the quotation marks. I finally responded, "Are you talking to me?"	31b
When the entire sentence—not the quotation—asks a question, place the question mark outside the quotation marks. Hadn't I read a sign that said, "Don't eat the fruit of the tree in the middle of the garden"?	31b
When a sentence ends with an abbreviation, the period also serves as the end punctuation for the sentence; never use two periods in succession. At this moment I noticed that it was 3:00 P.M.	31b
If a question ends with an abbreviation, add a question mark. Had I been in this garden since 11:00 A.M.?	31b

QUICK REFERENCE SUMMARY
CHAPTER 32
AVOIDING FRAGMENTS, FUSED SENTENCES, AND COMMA SPLICES

Rules and Examples	Section
An *independent clause* must contain a subject and a verb and must express a complete thought—it must not leave you hanging. **Not Independent Clause** Hoping to win a gold medal in the Olympics. (no subject) **Not Independent Clause** The woman throwing the shot put right now. (no verb) **Not Independent Clause** When Shannon Miller does the vault. (leaves you hanging) **Independent clause** <u>Subject</u> <u>Verb</u> Gwen Torrence was leading from the start of the race. (doesn't leave you hanging)	32a
A sentence must contain at least one independent clause and may contain more than one. **Sentence** <u>Independent clause</u> Kevin Young is favored in the 400-meter hurdles. **Sentence** <u>Independent clause</u> <u>Independent</u> He won this event in the 1992 Olympics, and he is in even better <u>clause</u> shape today. **Sentence** <u>Not independent clause</u> <u>Independent</u> If the volleyball team can win this game, they are guaranteed <u>clause</u> a bronze medal.	32a

Rules and Examples	Section
A *fragment* is a group of words that is punctuated as if it were a sentence when it is not; fragments are serious errors. **Fragment** Because television audiences prefer women's gymnastics to men's.	32b
A fragment occurs when a group of words has no subject. **Fragment** Taking incredible risks on the uneven bars.(no subject)	32b
A fragment occurs when a group of words has no verb. Remember that a verbal is *not* a verb. **Fragment** <u>verbal</u> The gymnast wearing a red, white, and blue lycra unitard. (no verb)	32b
A fragment occurs when a group of words is incomplete—leaves the reader hanging. **Fragment** When Dominique Daws began her floor routine. (leaves you hanging)	32b
The presence of one or more pronouns in a sentence does not make it *grammatically* incomplete, even though the sentence might not make complete sense in isolation. **Sentence** He cleared it with several inches to spare. *Even though we don't know who* he *is or what he* cleared, *this is* not *grammatically incomplete; it* is *a sentence.*	32b
Elliptical sentences are not fragments. <u>Sentence</u> <u>Sentence</u> Water polo players have to be in great shape. So do wrestlers. So do wrestlers *is a sentence. It is an* elliptical sentence, *meaning that words in the first sentence have been omitted from the second because they would be repetitious. In this case the omitted words are* have to be in great shape.	32b

Rules and Examples	Section
Fragments may be corrected in either of two ways. First, they can be joined to a nearby sentence. When runners get a good start in the 100-meter dash /, *T*hey have a distinct advantage.	32b

Second, fragments can be rewritten so that they are complete sentences.
    The captain of the Brazilian volleyball team was injured last night.
 	
    lost
The team ~~losing~~ the game by two points.
	32b

The serious error known as a *fused sentence* or *run-on sentence* occurs when you join two independent clauses without putting punctuation between them. **Fused sentence** <u>Independent clause</u> Tennis gets very little attention at the Summer Olympics fencing <u>Independent clause</u> gets even less.	32c
An equally serious error, a *comma splice*, occurs when you join two independent clauses with just a comma. **Comma splice** <u>Independent clause</u> <u>Independent clause</u> Handball does not get much attention, roller hockey gets none.	32c

To correct a fused sentence or comma splice, use one of the four options for joining independent clauses discussed in 33, or revise one of the clauses to make it dependent:
• Option 1: Use a period and a capital letter.
 	
                                     T
The Chinese 4 X 100 relay team runs well /. *T*hey should win a medal in the next Olympics.
• Option 2: Use a comma and a coordinating conjunction.
 	
                                     so
The Chinese 4 X 100 relay team runs well, they should win a medal in the next Olympics.
                                       ^
• Option 3: Use a semicolon.
 	
The Chinese 4 X 100 relay team runs well /; they should win a medal in the next Olympics.
	32c, 33a
	
	33a
	
	33b

Rules and Examples	Section
• Option 4: Use a semicolon and a conjunctive adverb. The Chinese 4 X 100 relay team runs well*; therefore,* they should win a medal in the next Olympics.	33c
• Or revise one of the clauses to make it dependent. *Because the* ~~The~~ ∧ Chinese 4 X 100 relay team runs well, they should win a medal in the next Olympics.	33d

QUICK REFERENCE SUMMARY
CHAPTER 33
USING COMMAS AND SEMICOLONS TO PUNCTUATE INDEPENDENT CLAUSES

Rules and Examples	Section
• Option 1: Separate independent clauses into two sentences. The Russian gymnast was not up to her usual standard today**.** She won only a bronze medal.	32c, 33a
• Option 2: Use a comma and a coordinating conjunction to join independent clauses. the Russian gymnast was not up to her usual standard today**,** but she won a bronze medal.	33a
• Option 3: Use a semicolon to join independent clauses. The Russian gymnast was not up to her usual standard today**;** she won only a bronze medal.	33b
• Option 4: Use a semicolon and a conjunctive adverb to join independent clauses. The Russian gymnast was not up to her usual standard today**;** nevertheless, she won a bronze medal.	33c

There are only seven coordinating conjunctions. Notice that they all have three letters or fewer.
    and   but   or   for
    so   yet   nor
	33a

Do not use a comma and a coordinating conjunction to join items that are not independent clauses; use the conjunction but not the comma in most of these cases. In the 200-meter freestyle race, one swimmer climbed up onto the starting block **/** and fell into the pool.	33b
If you are joining two independent clauses with a coordinating conjunction and one or both of the clauses also have internal commas, you may upgrade the comma between the clauses to a semicolon. Kim Zmeskal, who was expected to win a number of gold medals for gymnastics in 1992, was under a lot of pressure **/;** and she ended up doing very poorly.	33a
Use a semicolon before a conjunctive adverb only when you are joining independent clauses. Track and field involves many different sports**/,** for example, discus, javelin, the high jump, and the 100-yard dash.	33b

Rules and Examples	Section
Conjunctive adverbs must be set off by commas before and after them unless they appear at the beginning or end of an independent clause. The Olympics used to be for amateur athletes only; that rule, however, has changed.	33c
If you use a conjunctive adverb at the beginning of a clause, place a comma after but not before it. The Olympics used to be for amateur athletes only; however, that rule has changed.	33c
If you use a conjunctive adverb at the end of a clause, place a comma before but not after it. The Olympics used to be for amateur athletes only; that rule has changed, however.	33c
The most common conjunctive adverbs are listed below. accordingly for example in other words on the other hand after all for instance instead otherwise also further likewise similarly anyway furthermore meanwhile still as a result hence moreover subsequently besides however nevertheless then certainly in addition next thereafter consequently incidentally nonetheless therefore even so indeed of course thus finally in fact	33c

When you use a dependent clause with an independent clause that is joined to another independent clause, punctuate the dependent clause according to the rules in 34a; punctuate the independent clauses using one of the four options in 33.
 	
                    Dependent clause   *Independent*
When Ralph Ellison finished his second novel, he was living in
 	
        clause   *Independent clause*
Massachusetts, and his house caught on fire.
 	
            Independent clause   *Dependent*
He did not have a second copy because this was before the
 	
                clause   *Independent*
popularity of personal computers, and he has never
 	
        clause
rewritten the novel.
	33d

61

Rules and Examples	Section

Independent clause   *Independent*
Ellison has never written another novel, but his first novel is still
  clause   *Dependent clause*
very popular because it is beautifully written.
 	
            Independent clause
The second novel started with a boy being raised out of a coffin,
      Dependent clause   *Independent*
and when it reached the final chapter, an old man found a
       clause
coffin full of termites.	

On the following page you will find a chart that provides a visual summary of the conventions for punctuating independent clauses.

Punctuating Independent Clauses

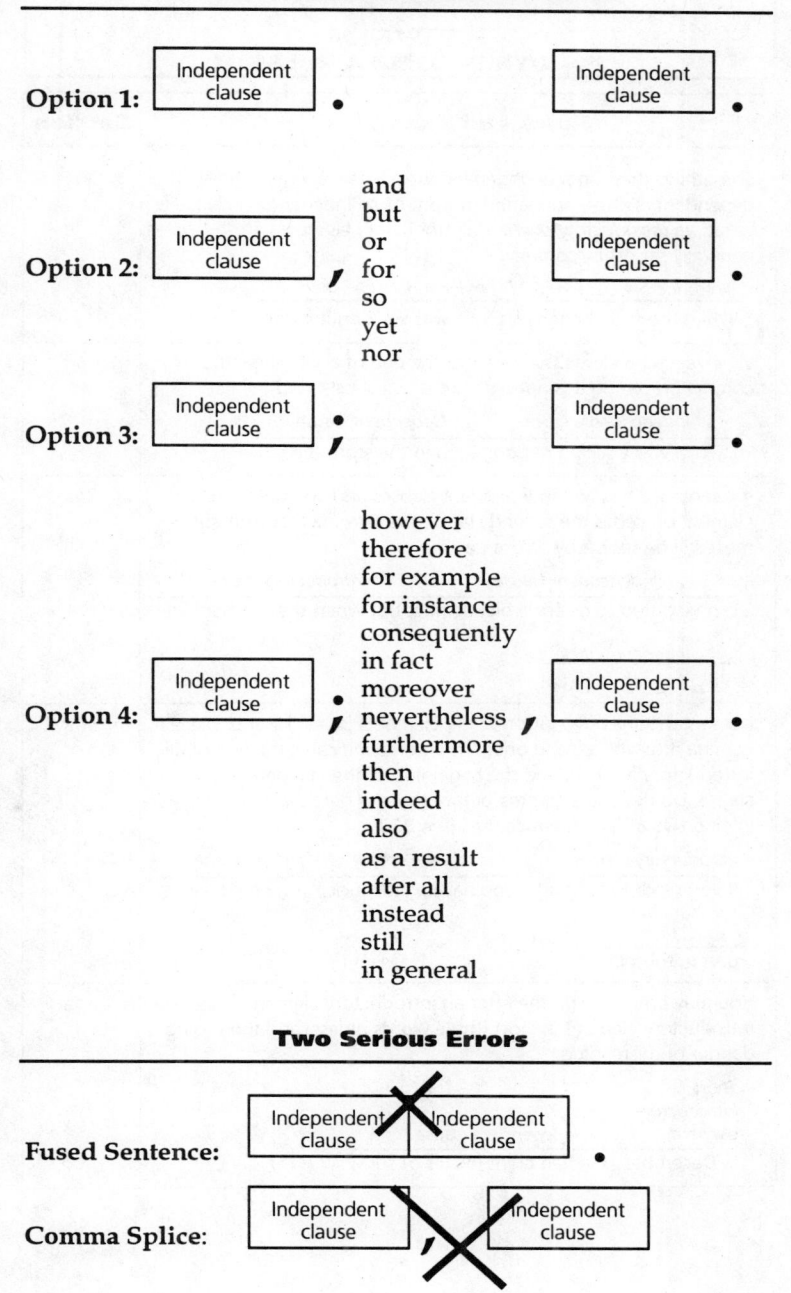

Option 1: [Independent clause] .   [Independent clause] .

Option 2: [Independent clause] , and / but / or / for / so / yet / nor [Independent clause] .

Option 3: [Independent clause] ; [Independent clause] .

Option 4: [Independent clause] ; however / therefore / for example / for instance / consequently / in fact / moreover / nevertheless / furthermore / then / indeed / also / as a result / after all / instead / still / in general , [Independent clause] .

Two Serious Errors

Fused Sentence: [Independent clause] [Independent clause] .

Comma Splice: [Independent clause] , [Independent clause] .

63

QUICK REFERENCE SUMMARY

CHAPTER 34
OTHER COMMA RULES

Rules and Examples	Section
Something that is not an independent clause—a word, phrase, or dependent clause—appearing in front of an independent clause is called an *introductory element*. Introductory elements are generally set off by commas. <u>Introductory element</u> <u>Independent clause</u> When the story began**,** LaToya was walking her dog.	34a
When such an element appears at the end of a sentence, the comma preceding it is optional but is usually omitted. <u>Independent clause</u> <u>Dependent clause</u> LaToya was walking her dog when the storm began.	34a

If a sentence has two independent clauses and an introductory element precedes the second clause, the introductory element must still be set off by a comma.
 	
   <u>Independent clause</u>   <u>Introductory element</u>
   Lynn wanted to go for a bicycle ride, but when she got her bike
 	
   <u>Independent clause</u>
   out**,** its tires were flat.
	34a

If a sentence has two introductory elements joined by *and*, place a comma after the second one. The comma indicates the end of all introductory material and the beginning of the independent clause. Do not use a comma before the *and* because it is not joining two independent clauses (see 33d).
 	
   <u>Introductory element</u>   <u>Introductory element</u>   <u>Independent</u>
   If you work hard and if you have a little luck**,** you could win a
 	
   <u>clause</u>
   part in this play.
	34a

You may omit the comma after an introductory element when the introductory element is short (three words or less) and there is no danger of misreading.
 	
   Short
   introductory
   <u>element</u>   <u>Independent clause</u>
   In December we had eight inches of snow.
	34a

Rules and Examples	Section
A word, phrase, or clause at the beginning of a sentence is not an introductory element *unless it is followed by an independent clause*. Do not use a comma after such an element if the rest of the sentence is not an independent clause. *Not independent clause* To drive to Kansas City takes about four hours.	34a
Items in a series are separated by commas. *Items in a series* Strawberries, blueberries, and plums are in season right now.	34b
The final comma—the one before the conjunction—is optional, but we recommend that you use it in order to eliminate any possibility of misreading. *Items in a series* The three puppies were gray, black and white, and brown.	34b
Never put a comma after the final item in a series. *Items in a series* Papers, books, and newspapers flew out of her car window.	34b
If the items in a series are long or contain internal commas of their own, you may use semicolons instead of commas to separate them. Recently more unusual fruit has come on the market such as the kiwi fruit, which originated in New Zealand; papayas, which are grown in Hawaii; and mangoes, which come from Mexico.	34b
Restrictive clauses or phrases narrow down or restrict the group of people or things a noun refers to; *nonrestrictive clauses or phrases* do not narrow down or restrict but only provide additional information about the noun they refer to. *Restrictive clause* The Chinese who live in Hong Kong have a high standard of living. *Nonrestrictive clause* The Chinese, who eat lots of rice and seafood, have a lower incidence of cancer than Americans.	34c

Rules and Examples	Section

Restrictive clauses or phrases are not set off by commas; nonrestrictive clauses or phrases are.
 	
    Restrictive clause
My friend who lives in Texas is coming to visit.
 	
    Nonrestrictive clause
My mother**,** who lives in Texas**,** is coming to visit.
	34c

A *parenthetical expression* is a phrase inserted in the middle of a sentence but not really a part of it. It is set off by commas.
 	
    Parenthetical
    expression
This camera**,** in my opinion**,** is overpriced.
	34d

A noun that is the name of the person being addressed and is not an integral part of the sentence is called a *noun of direct address*. It is set off by commas. *Noun* *of direct* *address* José**,** do you wish you were back in California?	34d
When you use *yes* or *no* at the beginning of a sentence, set it off with commas. Yes**,** I have gotten better at using commas since I read this book.	34d
Mild interjections should be set off by commas. *Mild* *interjection* Well**,** I suppose I should stay home and study this weekend.	34d
Tag questions are set off by commas. *Tag question* You were born in Hawaii**,** weren't you?	34d

When two adjectives are *coordinate,* each of them *separately* modifies the noun. Two adjectives are coordinate if you can insert the word *and* between them or if you can reverse their order without the sentence sounding odd.
 	
        Coordinate
        adjectives
Anneke was carrying a wet, muddy kitten into the kitchen.
 	
        Coordinate
        adjectives
Anneke was carrying a wet and muddy kitten into the kitchen.
	34e

Rules and Examples	Section
Coordinate <u>*adjectives*</u> Anneke was carrying a muddy, wet kitten into the kitchen.	34e

The second of two cumulative adjectives modifies the noun; the first modifies the combination of the second adjective and the noun. If you reverse two *cumulative* adjectives or insert *and* between them, the sentence sounds odd.
    Cumulative
    <u>*adjectives*</u>
The gray electric blanket was folded up at the end of the bed.
 	
Incorrect:
    Cumulative
    <u>*adjectives*</u>
The electric gray blanket was folded up at the end of the bed.
 	
Incorrect:
    Cumulative
    <u>*adjectives*</u>
The gray and electric blanket was folded up at the end of the bed.
	34e

Use a comma between coordinate adjectives (but no comma after the second one); do not use a comma between cumulative adjectives.
              Coordinate
              <u>*adjectives*</u>
The pilgrims made the long**,** difficult trip to Mecca.
 	
    Cumulative
    <u>*adjectives*</u>
The tall French woman is in my biology class.
	34e

An *absolute phrase* consists of a noun and the *-ed* or *-ing* form of a verb (past or present participle) and is used to modify the whole sentence rather than any specific word within it. It is set off by a comma. <u>*Absolute phrase*</u> Her homework finished**,** Lynn went for a bicycle ride.	34f

Rules and Examples	Section
A *contrasted element* is a phrase or clause set off from the rest of the sentence and introduced by a negative word such as *not, but,* or *unlike*. It is set off by commas. 　　　　　　　　　　　　　　　　　　　　　　Contrasted Mike explained that Paula is the one who is pregnant, not her element sister.	34g
Separate phrases like *said Arnie Becker, she replied, he said,* or *Emerson wrote* from quoted material with a comma. 　"Get out of here before I throw you out," said Arnie Becker.	34h
Do not use a comma to separate expressions like *he shouted* or *she said* from quoted material if the quotation ends with an exclamation point or question mark. 　"Sit down and be quiet!" he shouted.	34h
Quotations that are not introduced or followed by phrases like *said Arnie Becker, she replied, he said,* or *Emerson wrote* do not require commas. 　The principle that "opposites attract" was the basis of my parents' marriage.	34h
When the explanatory phrase like *said Arnie Becker, she replied, he said,* or *Emerson wrote* appears in the middle of a sentence, it is set off by commas. 　"My mother," said Francine, "does not sound like she is from the South."	34h
When the quoted material consists of more than one sentence and the explanatory phrase appears after the first sentence, use a comma to separate the quoted material from the explanatory phrase. Place a period after the phrase and start the next sentence of the quotation with a capital letter. 　"I am going to tell you of Sundiata," said the griot. "He was great among kings."	34h
In dates, use commas between the day and year and after the year. 　May 15, 1993, was a day I will always remember.	34i
If the year comes at the end of the sentence, follow it with a period rather than a comma. 　My mother was born on April 30, 1922.	34i
If you put the day of the week before a date, follow the day of the week with a comma. 　The warranty on my car expired on Monday, March 29, 1993.	34i

Rules and Examples	Section
If you invert the month and day (as is common in the military and in some businesses), do not use a comma. I was discharged from the army on 30 November 1988.	34i
When you use the month and year but not the day, a comma is not required. We recommend that you omit it. My loan will be paid off in December 1998.	34i
Use a comma between the city and state and after the state, unless the state is the last word in the sentence. Kansas City, Missouri, was our destination, not Kansas City, Kansas.	34i
Separate the items in an address with commas when it is written in sentence form, but do not use a comma between the state and zip code. Send your application to Nguyen Kao, 11308 South Shore Road, Stockton, California 95202.	34i
Even when no rule requires it, you should use a comma if it will help the reader avoid misreading a sentence. Students who are able to, write their papers on computers.	34j

Comma Rules
(Rules for using commas to punctuate independent clauses are covered in 33.)

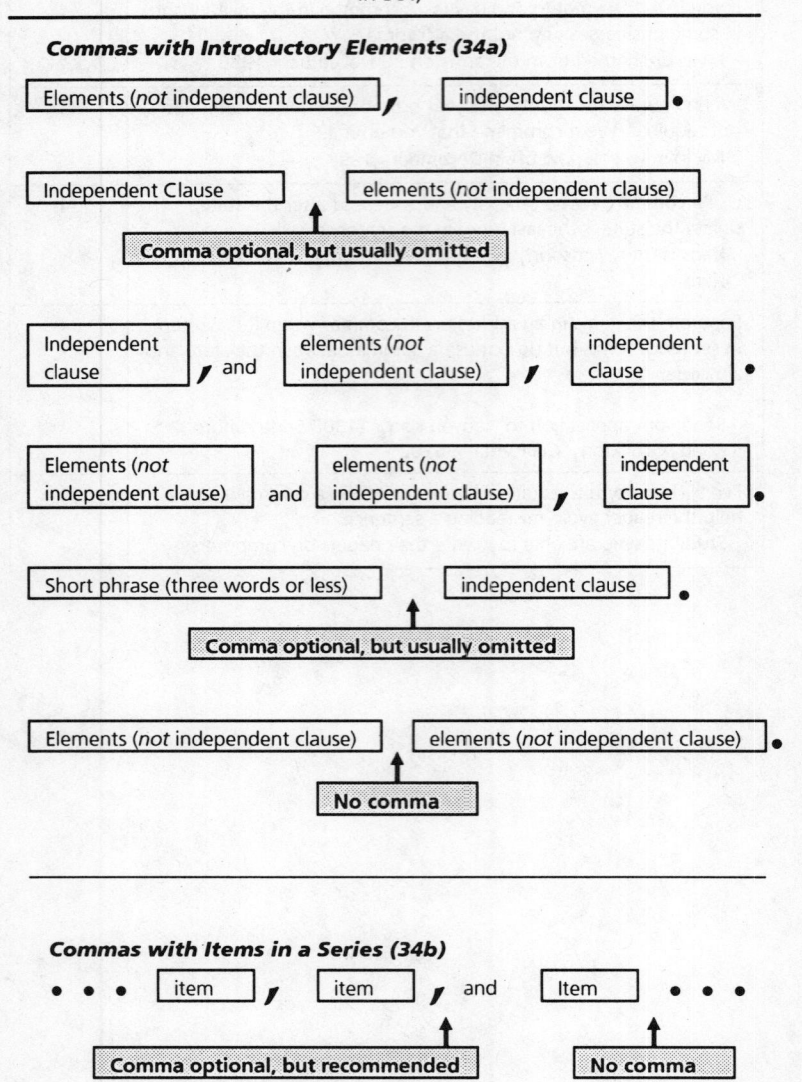

Commas with Introductory Elements (34a)

[Elements (*not* independent clause)] **,** [independent clause] **.**

[Independent Clause] [elements (*not* independent clause)]
↑ **Comma optional, but usually omitted**

[Independent clause] **,** and [elements (*not* independent clause)] **,** [independent clause] **.**

[Elements (*not* independent clause)] and [elements (*not* independent clause)] **,** [independent clause] **.**

[Short phrase (three words or less)] [independent clause] **.**
↑ **Comma optional, but usually omitted**

[Elements (*not* independent clause)] [elements (*not* independent clause)] **.**
↑ **No comma**

Commas with Items in a Series (34b)

• • • [item] **,** [item] **,** and [Item] • • •
↑ **Comma optional, but recommended** ↑ **No comma**

Commas with Restrictive and Nonrestrictive Clauses, Phrases, and Appositives (34c)

[Beginning of sentence] [restrictive element] [end of sentence] .

[Beginning of sentence] , [nonrestrictive element] , [end of sentence] .

Commas with Parenthetical Expressions (34d)

[Beginning of sentence] , [parenthetical expression] , [end of sentence] .

[Beginning of sentence] , [noun of direct address] , [end of sentence] .

[*Yes* or *No*] , [independent claue] .

[Interjection] , [independent clause] .

[independent clause] , [tag question] .

Commas with Coordinate and Cumulative Adjectives (34e)

• • • [coordinate adjective] , [coordinate adjective] [noun] • • •

• • • [cumulative adjective] [cumulative adjective] [noun] • • •

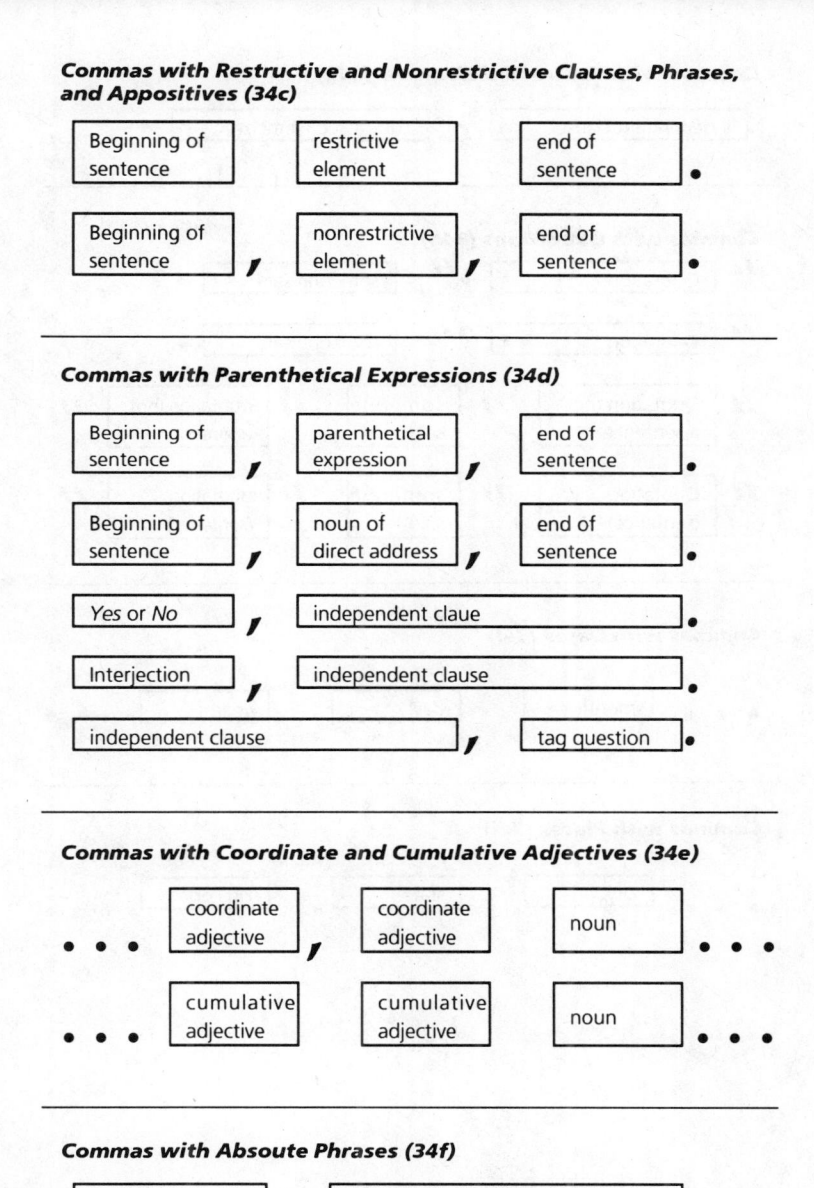

Commas with Absoute Phrases (34f)

[Absolute phrase] , [independent clause] .

Commas with Contrasted Elements (34g)

[Independent clause] , [contrasted element] .

Commas with Quotations (34h)

" [Quotation] ," [someone said] .

" [Quotation] ?" [someone said] .

" [Quotation (not a sentence)] ," [someone said] ," [quotation (not a sentence)] ."

" [Quotation (sentence)] ," [someone said] . " [quotation (sentence)] ."

Commas with Dates (34i)

. . . [month] [day] , [year] , . . .

Commas with Places (34i)

. . . [city] [state] , [zip code] , . . .

QUICK REFERENCE SUMMARY

CHAPTER 35
APOSTROPHES

Rules and Examples	Section
Nouns and pronouns are *possessive* when they indicate that something "belongs to" someone or something else. The following situations are considered *grammatically* possessive: 　Literal ownership　　　　　　Larry's car 　Parts of a person's body　　　Dr. Jimenez's eyes 　Relatives　　　　　　　　　　Suzie's mother 　A person's qualities or　　　　my sister's confidence 　　characteristics 　A person's products　　　　　Matisse's paintings 　Qualities or attributes of an　this company's record 　　organization 　People or things that are　　　tomorrow's leaders 　　being associated with 　　a certain period of time	35a
The following process will help you to form possessives correctly: 1. Ask yourself whether the word in question is possessing anything. Is it in a possessive situation? If not, do not make it possessive. 2. Ask yourself whether the word in question is a noun or indefinite pronoun (*someone, everybody*). If not, do not use an apostrophe and an *s* to make it possessive. Pronouns (except indefinite pronouns) never form their possessives with an apostrophe. 3. Ask yourself if the word is singular or plural. Write the word on scrap paper or in your head in its singular or plural form, as appropriate. Remember at this point that you are *only* making the word singular or plural; do *not* make it possessive until step 4. 4. Form the possessive as follows: 　a. If the word is singular, add an apostrophe and an -*s* ['s]. 　b. If the word is plural and ends in *s* add just an apostrophe [']. 　c. If the word is plural and ends in a letter other than an *s*, add an apostrophe and an -*s* ['s]. A chart summarizing this process can be found on page 76.	35a

Rules and Examples	Section
In the following special cases, you may vary the above procedure. • Singular words ending in *-s may* form their plurals by adding just an apostrophe, if the possessive ending is not pronounced as an additional syllable. Henry James's novel Moses' beard • Hyphenated words form their possessives by adding the apostrophe and an *-s* to the final word. my father-in-law's attitude • Groups of words that function as if they were a single word form their possessives by adding an apostrophe and an *-s* to the final word. the secretary of state's limousine • Nouns joined by *and* form their possessives in one of two ways: 1. If the two nouns own the thing *jointly,* that is, if it belongs to both of them, add an apostrophe and an *-s* to only the final noun. Harry and Esther's debts (The debts belong to both of them.) 2. If the two nouns own the things separately, add an apostrophe and an *-s* to *each* of the nouns. Harry's and Esther's debts (They each have separate debts.) • Nouns joined by *or* own the thing separately. Add an apostrophe and an *-s* to each noun. Charlie's and Mike's poem will win the prize.	35a
A pronoun does not form its possessive with an apostrophe and an *-s*. Instead, each pronoun has a slightly different form that is used for possessive situations. *his* My brother has lost ~~he's~~ wallet.	35b
In all but the most formal writing, use an apostrophe to join two words to form a contraction. *couldn't* Arki ~~could not~~ come to the meeting because she was baby-sitting for Mr. Jennings.	35c
In contractions, the apostrophe goes where one or more letters have been omitted, not where the two words are joined. *shouldn't* Nicole ~~should'nt~~ wear such expensive clothes.	35c

Forming Possessives

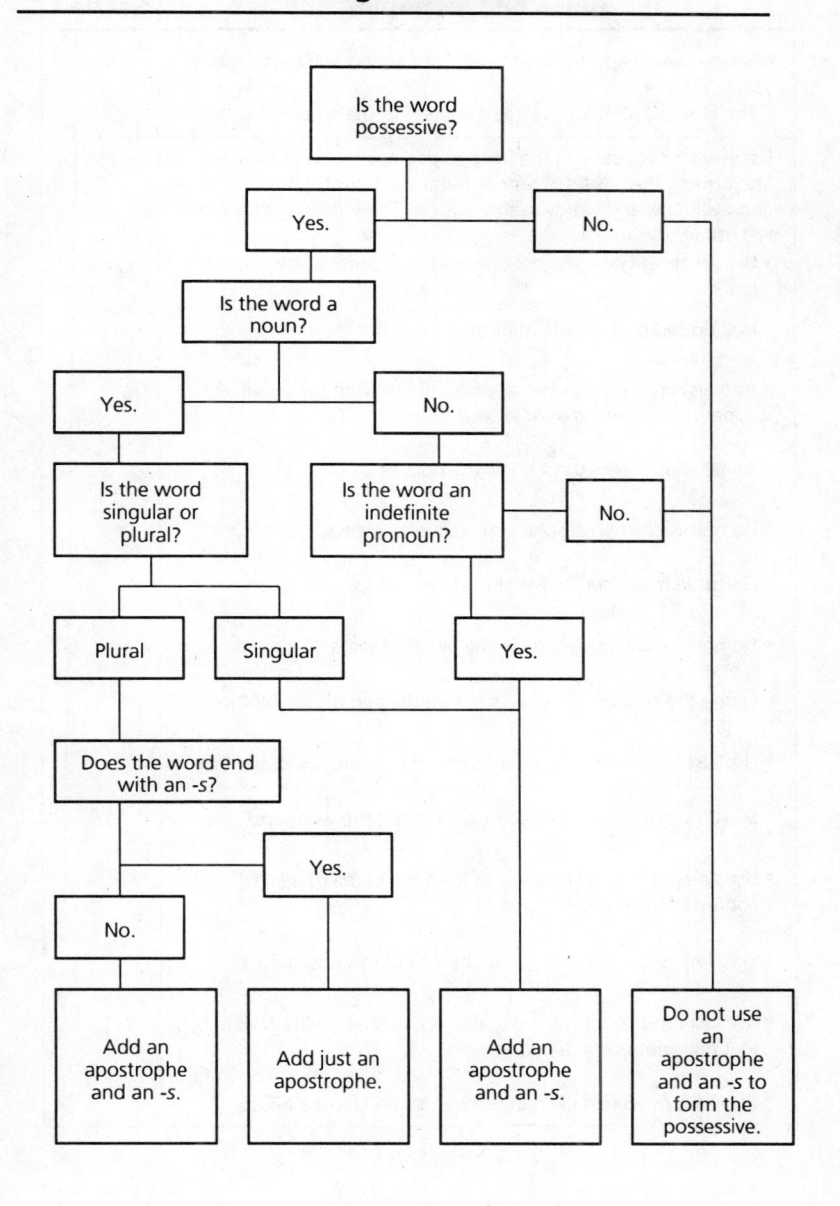

- Is the word possessive?
  - **No.** → Do not use an apostrophe and an -s to form the possessive.
  - **Yes.** → Is the word a noun?
    - **Yes.** → Is the word singular or plural?
      - **Plural** → Does the word end with an -s?
        - **No.** → Add an apostrophe and an -s.
        - **Yes.** → Add just an apostrophe.
      - **Singular** → Add an apostrophe and an -s.
    - **No.** → Is the word an indefinite pronoun?
      - **Yes.** → Add an apostrophe and an -s.
      - **No.** → Do not use an apostrophe and an -s to form the possessive.

Rules and Examples	Section
In years, use an apostrophe to indicate omitted numbers (usually *19*). The class of '92 made a large donation to the scholarship fund.	35c
Usage varies concerning the need to add apostrophes when you are forming the plurals of letters, numbers, symbols, abbreviations, and words used as words. The following guidelines will usually be correct. • Use an apostrophe and an -*s* to form the plural of lower-case letters. Ned dotted his *i*'s with little circles. • Add just an -*s* (without an apostrophe) to form the plural of upper-case letters used as letters. Angela had received A's on all the quizzes. • Do not use an apostrophe in plurals of numbers. Gertrude made her 7's with little cross marks. • Do not use an apostrophe in the plural of years. I hope the economy improves before the end of the 1990s. • Use just an -*s* to form the plural of symbols such as & and $. She always used &'s instead of writing out the word *and*. • Use an apostrophe and an -*s* to form the plural of an abbreviation ending in a period. Very few R.N.'s work on the night shift at this hospital. • Use just an -*s* to form the plural of an upper-case abbreviation that does not end in a period. Two BMWs were parked in front of Nancy Hume's house.	35d

Rules and Examples	Section
• Use an apostrophe and an -s to form the plural of a lower-case abbreviation. Professor Schwartz's collection of lp*'s* from the 1950s was destroyed in the fire. • Use an apostrophe and an -s to form the plural of a word when it is used to represent itself. The opening paragraph of Donna's essay contained five *'s* consequently.	35d
Do not confuse contractions and possessives of pronouns. Remember that pronouns (except indefinite pronouns) never use apostrophes to form possessives. Be especially careful with the following pairs: *its/it's, your/you're, their/they're, whose/who's.* *its* My dog was chasing ~~it's~~ tail. *you're* Make sure ~~your~~ registered for the course. *their* I lost ~~they're~~ tickets for the game. *who's* Vivian doesn't know ~~whose~~ coming to the party.	35e
Do not use apostrophes with nouns that are plural but not possessive. *boats* Three ~~boat's~~ were wrecked by the storm.	35e

QUICK REFERENCE SUMMARY

**CHAPTER 36
QUOTATION MARKS**

Rules and Examples	Section
A direct quotation reproduces the *exact* words someone has spoken or written. 　In *No Easy Walk to Freedom,* Nelson Mandela wrote, "I have fought against White domination, and I have fought against Black domination" (189).	36a
An indirect quotation tells what someone said or wrote, but with changes in tense and person to make the passage fit more smoothly into your sentence. 　In *No Easy Walk to Freedom,* Nelson Mandela wrote that he had fought against White domination, and he had fought against Black domination (189).	36a
A paraphrase tells what someone said or wrote, but expressed completely in your words. 　In *No Easy Walk to Freedom,* Nelson Mandela wrote that he had opposed both black and white domination (189).	36a
Use quotation marks to mark the beginning and the end of each section of directly quoted text. 　"To be equal to men," writes Marilyn French, "does not mean to be like them."	36a
Quoted material that is longer than four lines, according to the MLA guidelines, should be set off by moving the left margin in ten spaces and double-spacing the text. If you are following other guidelines (like APA), consult those for specifics. Do not use quotation marks with such indented text. 　See example in text.	36b
Place short quotations of poetry (three lines or less) within the text. Use quotation marks at the beginning and end and separate lines with a slash (/). Be sure to leave a space on either side of the slash. 　When Robert Frost wrote, "The woods are lovely, dark and deep, / But I have promises to keep," I think he was explaining why he would not consider suicide.	36b
Longer quotations of poetry (more than three lines) should be indented ten spaces and double-spaced according to MLA guidelines. If you are following other guidelines (like APA), consult them for specifics. Do not use quotation marks, but do attempt to recreate the look of the poem on the page. 　See example in text.	36b

Rules and Examples	Section
When reproducing dialogue, place the words of each speaker in quotation marks and start a new paragraph each time the speaker changes. Set off phrases like *he said* and *Matt replied* with commas. See example in text.	36c
When a quotation occurs within a quotation, the inner quotation is set off with *single* rather than double quotation marks. In his book *Working,* Studs Terkel describes Dolores Dante, a waitress whose "pride in her skills helps her make it through the night. 'When I put the plate down, you don't hear a sound.' "	36d
Set off titles of short works with quotation marks (but no commas). Short works include short stories, most poems, one-act plays, chapters, articles, essays, songs, and episodes of radio or television programs. I've just finished reading "O Yes" by Tillie Olsen.	36e
Words used as words are usually italicized (underlined) but may be placed in quotation marks instead. Whichever option you choose, be consistent within a single piece of writing. Professor Curmudgeon used "hegemony" fourteen times in her speech yesterday.	36f
Words used ironically are placed in quotations marks. Alvin's "limousine" was actually a Volkswagen Rabbit.	36g
Definitions of words may be set off with quotation marks. Ms. Lewis is using *affect* to mean "a feeling or emotion."	36h

Periods go *inside* of quotation marks except when a parenthetical citation follows the quotation.
 	
   My aunt said, "I believe that Malcolm X was a great leader."
   "Greek philosophy began with three men from Miletus" (Barnes 36).
	36j

Commas always go *inside* of quotation marks. "Here is the light switch," shouted Mr. Chang.	36j
Colons and semicolons always go *outside* of quotation marks. The letter from the Department of Motor Vehicles said, "You owe a total of $129 for overdue fines"; I've never gotten a ticket in my life, so I know there is some mistake.	36j

Rules and Examples	Section

Place the question mark inside the quotation marks when the quoted words are a question; place it outside the quotation marks when the whole sentence is a question.
  Nan asked, "What did you get on the test?"
 	
  Did Joan say, "I don't care about grades"?
	36j

Place the exclamation point inside the quotation marks if it applies to the quoted material and outside if it applies to the whole sentence.
  When the couch fell on her foot, Coretta shouted one word, "Damn!"
  I will never use the words "I give up"!
	36j

Place dashes inside the quotation marks if they clearly belong to the quoted material; otherwise, place them outside.
  "I will not open my—" began Mitchel, until Carry's look silenced him.
  Peter said to the teacher, "I missed the final exam because my grandmother died"—the oldest excuse in the book.
	36j

QUICK REFERENCE SUMMARY

CHAPTER 37
OTHER PUNCTUATION MARKS

Rules and Examples	Section

A colon is a fairly formal punctuation mark used following an independent clause to indicate a greater break between grammatical elements than a semicolon, but less than a period. The second element is usually an illustration or amplification of the initial independent clause and may be any of the following.
• A word
   There was one explanation for her success: luck.
• A phrase
   Max was hiding in the one place we never thought to look: under his bed.
• A list
   My collection included three kinds of recipes: salads, appetizers, and desserts.
• A quotation
   You should remember what Thoreau said about being in jail: "Under a government which imprisons any unjustly, the true place for a just man is also in prison."
• An independent clause
   The teacher did the only thing he could under the circumstances: he dismissed class.
	37a

Starting an independent clause that follows a colon with a capital letter is optional, unless the colon is followed by a quoted sentence, which must begin with a capital letter.
   Jake did the one thing he could do: he ran out of the room.
   Jake did the one thing he could do: He ran out of the room.
   President Kennedy's words echoed in my ears: "Ask not what your country can do for you, but what you can do for your country."
	37a

Do not use a colon after an element that is not an independent clause.
   A colon would be wrong here. ⎯⎯⎯┐
   The two aspects of yoga we teach are *pranayama* and *asana*.
	37a

Rules and Examples	Section
Also, use a colon • To separate the hour and minutes in time 　The train arrived at 6:38 P.M. • To separate the salutation of a business letter from the body of the letter 　Dear Sir or Madam: • To separate the two parts of a title 　The text for my psychology course is *Understanding Human Behavior: An Introduction to Behavioral Psychology.* • To separate the two terms in a ratio or proportion 　The ratio of water to salt is 10:1 in this solution.	37a
Use either a period or a colon to separate the chapter number from the verse in references to the Bible. We recommend using a period. 　We preferred the version of creation in Genesis 1.27 to that in Genesis 2.22. 　We preferred the version of creation in Genesis 1:27 to that in Genesis 2:22.	37a
An *ellipsis* is a series of three periods separated by spaces used to indicate that some material has been left out in a direct quotation. Use an ellipsis to indicate where words have been omitted from the original. 　Annie Dillard tells about hiding a penny in the sidewalk near her home in Pittsburgh. "Then I would take a piece of chalk, and . . . draw huge arrows leading up to the penny from both directions" (14).	37b
An ellipsis is *not* used to indicate the omitted material at the beginning of a quotation. When an omission at the end of a quotation coincides with the end of the writer's sentence, a period (to indicate the end of the sentence) is placed immediately after the final word; this period is then followed by a traditional ellipsis (three spaced periods). 　After hiding her penny, Dillard reports that she never waited to see who would find it, but "would go straight home and not give the matter another thought. . . ." *(Note that this quotation does not include a citation; the next one does.)*	37b

Rules and Examples	Section
When the end of the quotation coincides with the end of the sentence and the writer includes a citation (see 46d), the final period is placed after the citation. Note that no space follows the final period of the three spaced periods making up the ellipsis. Telling about her childhood prank of hiding a penny and then marking the path to it with arrows, Annie Dillard observes that she "was greatly excited, during all this arrow-drawing . . ." (Dillard 14).	37b
If an entire sentence is omitted and if the omission is preceded and followed by complete sentences, use a four-dot ellipsis. Annie Dillard tells a story about a curious activity she engaged in when she was a child. "When I was six or seven years old, growing up in Pittsburgh, I used to take a precious penny of my own and hide it for someone else to find. . . . For some reason I always 'hid' the penny along the same stretch of sidewalk up the street" (14).	37b

In quoted poetry of more than three lines, a full line of spaced periods is used to indicate the omission of one or more lines of the original poem.
    Let me not to the marriage of true minds
    Admit impediment. Love is not love
    Which alters when it alteration finds
    Or bends with the remover to remove
    . . . .
    Love alters not with his brief hours and weeks,
    But bears it out even to the edge of doom.
    If this be error and upon me proved,
    I never writ, nor no man ever loved.
                    —Shakespeare, Sonnet 116
	37b

An ellipsis may be used to indicate a hesitation or interruption in the words of a speaker or writer or to suggest speech or writing left unfinished. I wonder what would happen . . .	37b
Use *parentheses* to set off information that is supplementary to the main idea of the sentence. Mayor Schmidt (my uncle) announced a 20 percent budget cut.	37c
Introduce the reader to an acronym or abbreviation by first using the spelled-out name and including the acronym in parentheses. In later references to the organization, just the acronym can be used. The Modern Language Association (MLA) publishes a guide to research and documentation.	37c

Rules and Examples	Section
In business writing, it is common to spell out amounts of money and then to indicate the same amount parenthetically in numbers. The interest on this debt amounts to six thousand four hundred dollars ($6400) per year.	37c
When presenting a numbered or lettered list, it is conventional to place the numbers or letters in parentheses. The causes of the accident were (1) excessive speed, (2) faulty brakes, and (3) foggy conditions.	37c
When an entire sentence appears in parentheses, begin the sentence with a capital letter and end it with a period. do not place an entire sentence in parentheses within another sentence. My mother never learned to drive an automobile. (She grew up in rural China.) She did, however, get her pilot's license in 1972.	37c
Use parentheses to set off citations indicating the sources of quotations and paraphrases in your writing. (See 46d.) Wagenknecht reports that Hawthorne's father "died, at twenty-eight, when his son was only four years old . . ." (1).	37c
Use *brackets* to indicate places within direct quotations where the writer has inserted material or made minor changes in the wording. John Dean reports that "within a month of coming to the White House, [he] had crossed an ethical line."	37d
When material already inside parentheses needs to be placed inside parentheses, use brackets instead. I had to meet with a representative of the neighborhood organization (a man who was rumored to work for the Central Intelligence Agency [CIA] and whom I had avoided for years).	37d
Use *dashes* to set off parenthetical information *that you want to emphasize*. If you are using a typewriter, two hyphens represent a dash. The President—with only three weeks remaining in his term—should not appoint a new Supreme Court justice.	37e
Dashes are also used to indicate breaks in sentences, discontinuities of thought. Frank returned slowly to the study—a room he had added to the house only three years earlier.	37e
The *slash* is used to separate lines of poetry when they are within the text. Add a space before and after the slash. (See 36b for more discussion of quoting poetry.) Poet Emily Dickinson's self-effacing style can be seen in her lines, "I'm nobody. Who are you? / Are you nobody too?"	37f

Rules and Examples	Section
The slash is also used to form fractions. 　　An error of 1/32 of a millimeter can make the tool inoperable.	37f
In informal or brief communications, use slashes to form dates. 　　The memoir was dated 3/12/93.	37f
Two words may be joined by a slash to indicate that either is appropriate. 　　Your mother and / or your father may also attend the banquet.	37f
To avoid sexism, the third-person pronoun is sometimes written *he/she* or *s/he*, indicating that it is referring to either a man or a woman; however, many readers find this use clumsy. We recommend that you use *he or she* instead. 　　A student should always make sure he / she understands an assignment before beginning to work on it.	37f

QUICK REFERENCE SUMMARY

CHAPTER 38
CAPITALIZATION

Rules and Examples	Section
Capitalize the first word in every sentence. This coffee is great.	38a
Begin each line of a poem with a capital letter, unless the poet chose not to. Rest at pale evening . . . A tall, slim tree . . . Night coming tenderly Black like me. 　　　　Langston Hughes, "Dream Variations"	38a
When an independent clause follows a colon, begin the independent clause with either an upper- or a lower-case letter, but be consistent. Polly is a determined woman: she went back to college at the age of forty-five. Polly is a determined woman: She went back to college at the age of forty-five.	38a
If a *quoted* sentence follows a colon, it must begin with a capital letter. 　　　　　　　　　　　　　　　　　　*A* President Kennedy's words echoed in my ears: Ask not what your country can do for you, but what you can do for your country."	38a
When a colon introduces material that consists of more than one sentence, each sentence must begin with a capital letter, including the one following the colon. 　　　　　　　　　　　　　　　*H* Bruce acted erratically after the accident: He jumped out of his car. He started shouting at passing cars. Then he lay down on the shoulder of the road and went to sleep.	38a
Capitalize proper nouns, that is, nouns that are the *names* of specific persons, places, or things. A proper noun must not only *refer* to a specific person, place, or thing, it must be the *name* of that specific person, place, or thing.	38b

Rules and Examples	Section

Capitalize people's names and titles that are used with names; do not capitalize titles used without names.
    Tracey Robertson   a freshman
    Professor Scheper   the professor
    Dean Snope   the dean
	38b

Capitalize *names* of groups based on racial, religious, national, or ethnic identity. Do no capitalize words that apply to groups but are not their names.
    African American   aborigine
    Black   disabled
    Chicano   minority
    Jew   northerner
    Native American   yuppie
    White
	38b

Capitalize names of specific places, including terms like *river, state,* or *ocean* when they are used with the place name. Do not capitalize terms like *river, state,* or *ocean* when they are used alone. Do not capitalize words like *south* or *east* when they indicate direction.
    Indian Ocean   the ocean
    Delaware River   the river
    the State of California   this state
    the South   walking south
	38b

Capitalize names of organizations, including words like *company, college,* and *department* when they are used as part of the name; do not capitalize generic words like *company, college,* and *department* when they are used alone.
    Eastman Kodak Company   the company
    Miami Dade Community College the college
    the Department of Psychology   the psychology department
	38b

Capitalize terms for historical periods that have developed an individual identity like the *Roaring Twenties* or the *Middle Ages,* but lower-case other terms that are more generic. If in doubt, consult a dictionary.
    the Vietnam War   the war
    the Age of Enlightenment the eighteenth century
    the Roaring Twenties   the sixties
	38b

Capitalize names of days of the week and months, but not seasons or numbers that represent particular dates.
    Wednesday   winter
    March   the thirteenth of June
	38b

Rules and Examples	Section

Capitalize names for the deity and titles of sacred books in all religions, but not the generic terms *god* and *goddess*.
  God   a statue of a god
  Allah   a painting of a goddess
  the Talmud   a hymnal
	38b

In scientific names of plants and animals, the genus is capitalized, and the species is lower-cased. Vernacular (everyday) names for plants and animals are lower-cased, unless they include a proper noun.
  Homo sapiens   oak tree
  Ipomoea tricolor   iris
                                German shepherd
	38b

Names of heavenly bodies are capitalized; words that stand for heavenly bodies but are not names are lower-cased. *Earth, sun,* and *moon* are generally not capitalized; however, when they are used in a discussion of other capitalized heavenly bodies, they frequently are.
  Mars   planet
  Venus   star
  Crab Nebula   galaxy
	38b

Words referring to chemicals, scientific laws, or diseases are not considered names and so are not capitalized, except for proper nouns or adjectives like *Newton* and *Kaposi's*.
  Newton's second law   uranium
  Kaposi's sarcoma   the second law of thermo-
                                   dynamics
                                   cancer
	38b

Registered trade names should be capitalized, but generic names should not. If in doubt, check a dictionary.
  Kleenex   tissues
  Advil   aspirin
  Xerox   photocopier
	38b

Capitalize names of specific courses, but not words that describe subject areas, unless they include words (like *Russian* or *Greek*) that are derived from proper nouns. *English* is capitalized even when it refers only to a general subject area because it is a proper adjective.
  Sociology 101   psychology
  Early Childhood Psychology   physics
  Review Mathematics   Russian history
                                  Greek drama
	38b

Rules and Examples	Section

Capitalize proper adjectives, that is, adjectives that are derived from proper nouns.
    French   Shakespearean
    Roman   Christian
    Asian   Jewish
	38c

Capitalize the pronoun *I* and the interjection *O*.
    When I heard the phone ring, I answered it.
    I replied, "I will do whatever you wish, O mighty one."
	38d

Capitalize the first words of quotations that are sentences by themselves.
    My father said, "Be home by midnight," as we walked out the door. (Quotation *is* a sentence by itself.)
    My father asked us not to "besmirch the family's name." (Quotation is *not* a sentence by itself.)
	38e

Capitalize the main words in titles. Articles, prepositions, coordinating conjunctions, and the *to* in infinitives are not capitalized (regardless of their length) unless they are the first or last words of the title or subtitle.
    The Floating Opera
    Sundiata: An Epic of Old Mali
    "The Artist of the Beautiful"
	38e

The style for capitalizing a series of questions that are not complete sentences varies. Use the style you prefer, but be consistent throughout a single piece of writing.
    What will the government tax next? Our children? Our underwear? Our garbage?
    What will the government tax next? our children? our underwear? our garbage?
	38g

QUICK REFERENCE SUMMARY

CHAPTER 39
ABBREVIATIONS AND ACRONYMS

Rules and Examples	Section

Common personal and professional titles are normally abbreviated.
  Ms. Hillary Clinton   Dr. Marie Williams
  George Scheper, Ph.D.   Nancy Hume, M.A.
  Henry Wadsworth, Jr.   Kent G. Stockdale III
	39a

The abbreviated forms of common titles, including religious, military, academic, and government titles, may be used before the person's full name; use the full title, however, before the last name only. In most academic writing, titles should be spelled out even when the full name is given.
  Prof. Ralph Stephen   Professor Stephens
  Sen. Barbara Boxer   Senator Boxer
  Col. L. Dow Adams   Colonel Adams
	39a

Do not use titles both before and after a name; choose one or the other.
  Professor Lynda Salamon, ~~Ph.D.~~
  ~~Mr.~~ Stephen Howard, Ph.D.
	39a

Do not use abbreviations for titles when they appear in text without a name. I explained to my ~~prof.~~ *professor* that I had an appointment with my ~~Dr.~~ *doctor*	39a
Typesetters normally use *small caps*—letters the size of lower-case letters but in the form of capital letters—for A.M. or P.M.; if your typewriter or computer doesn't have small capitals, use lower-case letters. 10:30 P.M. or 10:30 p.m.	39b

Use small capitals, if you can, for A.D. and B.C.; if small capitals are not available, use *upper-case* letters for A.D. and B.C. B.C. follows the date; A.D. precedes it.
  400 B.C. or 400 B.C.
  A.D. 1492 or A.D. 1492
	39b

B.C.E. stands for "before the common era" and means the same as B.C. It is used to avoid the Christian significance of B.C. 400 B.C.E. or 400 B.C.E.	39b

Rules and Examples	Section
C.E. stands for "common era" and means the same as A.D. It is used to avoid the Christian significance of A.D. Notice that C.E. follows the date than preceding it, as A.D. does. 1492 C.E. or 1492 C.E.	39b

The abbreviation for *number* may be either capitalized or lower-cased.
  No. 10 Downing Street
  no. 10 Downing Street
	39b

Use a dollar sign with numbers and a decimal point to indicate the division between dollar and cent amounts. $19.95	39b
A small circle in the superscript position stands for the word *degrees*. A capital *F* indicates that the temperature is being measured on the Fahrenheit scale; a capital *C* indicates that the Celsius (centigrade) scale is being used. The K without degree mark indicates a temperature on the Kelvin scale. 32°F 43°C 100 K	39b

Abbreviations of organizations, companies, and government agencies are acceptable in most writing; today they are most commonly used without periods.
  CIA   the Central Intelligence Agency
  NAACP the National Association for the Advancement of Colored People
  IBM   International Business Machines
  NOW   National Organization for Women
	39c

In general, avoid Latin terms and the abbreviations for them in your writing. These are reserved primarily for use in documenting sources (see 46).
  cf.   compare (*confer*)
  e.g.   for example (*exempli gratia*)
  et al.   and others (*et alii*)
  i.e.   that is (*id est*)
	39d

In general, true abbreviations—that is, single words shortened by the omission of letters—are followed by a period. St. Blvd. Nov.	39e
An *acronym* consists of the first letters of a series of words in a name used as a shortened version of that name. It is pronounced as though it were a word and generally appears without periods. CARE UNICEF MIRV	39e

Rules and Examples	Section
Initial abbreviations, which are made up of the first letters of a series of words in a name and are pronounced by saying each letter, are also commonly written without periods. 　IRS　　　　IBM　　　　　　AFL–CIO	39e
When periods are used with abbreviations, do not put a space between the period and the next letter. 　A.M.　　　U.S.A.　　　　　B.C.	39e

QUICK REFERENCE SUMMARY

CHAPTER 40
NUMBERS

Rules and Examples	
In writing that includes few numbers, use words for all numbers that can be expressed in one or two words. six fourteen twenty-one ninety-nine one thousand	40
In writing that includes few numbers, use numerals for numbers that require three or more words. 104 128 1,352	40
In writing that includes many numbers, use words for the numbers *one* to *nine*. one six nine	40
In writing that includes many numbers, use numerals for all numbers other than those from *one* to *nine*. 10 45 100 1,000	40

When you do write out lengthy numbers in words, use *and* only to indicate the place where a decimal point would go; do not use *and* between the "hundreds" and the "tens" in a number.
    one hundred ~~and~~ twenty-two
 	
    thirty-one and nine-tenths
	40

When you use words for numbers from *twenty-one* to *ninety-nine*, hyphenate the two words. thirty-six fifty-eight	40

Do not begin a sentence with a number expressed in numerals. Either write the number in words or recast the sentence so the number appears later.
    One hundred twenty-six
    ~~126~~ people applied for this job.
 	
    There were 126 applicants for this job.
    ~~126 people applied for this job.~~
	40

93

QUICK REFERENCE SUMMARY

CHAPTER 41
ITALICS

Rules and Examples	Section

Use italic type or underlining to indicate the titles of book-length works and longer works in the visual and musical arts.
  Books   *A Brief History of Time*
  Plays   *King Lear*
  Long Musical Works   Haydn's *Creation*
  Long Poems   Eliot's *The Waste Land*
  Visual Art   Matisse's *Pink Nude*
  Magazines   the *Atlantic Monthly*
  Newspapers   the *St. Louis Post-Dispatch*
  Television Programs   *60 minutes*
  Films   *Rebel without a Cause*
  Journals   *Modern Fiction Studies*
	41a

Legal documents, religious books such as the Bible or the Koran, and parts of these works are *not* italicized, underlined, or placed in quotations marks.
  the Bible   the Declaration of Independence
  the Talmud   the Book of Job
	41a

If italics are not available, underline those words that you would otherwise italicize; underlining has exactly the same meaning as italicizing text. <u>The Bluest Eye</u> <u>A Brief History of Time</u> <u>King Lear</u> <u>Paradise Lost</u>	41a
The *names* of spacecraft, ships, airplanes, and trains are italicized or underlined. *Challenger* the *Titanic*	41b

Use italics or underlining to indicate a word, letter, or number used, not with its normal meaning, but because you are discussing it *as a word, letter, or number*.
  My boss uses *advice* the way other people use *command*.
  A small circle appeared above each *i* that she wrote.
  There was an extra *8* in her equation.
	41c

Whey they are used in English sentences, foreign words are italicized or underlined.
  Adios was all she said as she drove away.
  He led the life of a *bon vivant*.
	41d

Rules and Examples	Section
Italics or underlining may be used to indicate stress or emphasis on a word or phrase. I can't believe that *you* did that.	41e

QUICK REFERENCE SUMMARY

CHAPTER 42
HYPHENS

Rules and Examples	Section
Use a hyphen to divide a word at the end of the line when there isn't room for the entire word. Lynn McCann checked into the Refuge Motor Inn on Chinco- teague Island.	42a

Divide words only between syllables.
                                                          tempera-
    Molly said that the forecast for the next day was for ~~temperatu-~~
tures
~~res~~ in the high eighties.
	42a

Never divide one-syllable words. When she came to the beach, Lynn brought towels and a ~~lar-~~ *large* ~~ge~~ supply of good books.	42a
When you divide a word, never leave a single letter at the end of one line, nor fewer than three letters at the beginning of the next line. Lynn put on her swimming suit, threw a large pink towel ~~a-~~ *around* ~~round~~ her shoulders, and headed for the beach.	42a
When you are dividing a word that is already hyphenated, always divide it at the hyphen. Thinking about how much she had spent on her fancy soft-~~sid-~~ *sided* ~~ed~~ luggage, the cost of the room for the week, and the expense of eating all her meals in restaurants did not dampen her joy.	42a

Compound words take three different forms: words that are run together, hyphenated words, and two words. Use the correct form (when in doubt, check your dictionary).
    blueberry   blue-collar   blue cheese
    crosswalk   cross-reference   cross section
	42b

When two or more adjectives modify a noun as a unit, they should be hyphenated.
    a well-known actor   an English-speaking tour guide
    a blood-curdling scream   a sloppy-looking paper
	42c

96

Rules and Examples	Section

When two or more adjectives come after the noun, they are not hyphenated even if they are used as a unit.
  That actor is not well known.
  Tyrone's paper was well written.
	42c

Adverbs ending in -*ly* are not hyphenated.
  a carefully ironed shirt
  a slowly moving truck
	42c

Words in comparative or superlative forms (see 28c) are not hyphenated.
  the most expensive ring
  a less provocative position
	42c

Use a hyphen for two-word numbers between twenty-one and ninety-nine.
  twenty-one   eighty-six
  fifty-five   ninety-nine
	42d

When you are expressing fractions in words, use a hyphen between the numerator and the denominator.
  one-half   three-fourths
  four-hundredths   seven-eighths
	42d

Do not use a hyphen between the numerator and denominator if either of them contains hyphens.
  three thirty-seconds
  sixty-four hundredths
	42d

Use a hyphen with the prefixes *self-*, *all*, *ex-* (when it means "former"), and *quasi-* and with the suffix *-elect*.
  self-confident   self-employed
  ex-wife   quasi-official
  president-elect   all-inclusive
	42e

Hyphenate prefixes when either the base word or the prefix begins with a capital letter.
  un-American   post-Reagan era
  A-frame   non-African
	42e

Sometimes a hyphen is used to prevent misreading.
  re-creation   recreation
  re-cover   recover
	42e

Rules and Examples	Section

When two or more prefixes are used to modify the same word, each prefix retains its hyphen even though the base word appears only once.
   full- and part-time employees
   pre- and post-surgery procedures
   English- or Chinese-speaking students
   two- and four-year colleges
	42f

QUICK REFERENCE SUMMARY

CHAPTER 44
SPELLING

Rule 1: *i* before *e* except after *c* or when sounded like *ay* as in *neighbor* or *weigh*.

Examples
belief	niece	chief
receipt	receive	deceive
eight	neigh	sleigh

Exceptions
either	leisure	seize
foreign	neither	their
height	protein	weird

Rule 2: When a suffix that begins with a vowel (like *-er*, *-est*, *-ed*, or *-ing*) is added to a word, the consonant is doubled if all of the following are true.

1. The word ends in a single consonant.
2. The final consonant is preceded by a single vowel.
3. The accent (stress) is on the last syllable (or the word has only one syllable).

Examples
occur	+	ed	=	occurred
run	+	ing	=	running
refer	+	ing	=	referring
begin	+	ing	=	beginning
sleep	+	ing	=	sleeping
benefit	+	ing	=	benefiting
listen	+	ing	=	listening
fight	+	ing	=	fighting

Exceptions
mortal	+	ly	=	mortally
room	+	mate	=	roommate
rotten	+	ness	=	rottenness
usual	+	ly	=	usually

Rule 3: When words end in a silent -e, the -e is dropped before adding a suffix that begins with a vowel. The -e is retained before a suffix that begins with a consonant.

Examples

require	+	ing	=	requiring
oblige	+	ation	=	obligation
tribe	+	al	=	tribal
require	+	ment	=	requirement
force	+	ful	=	forceful
like	+	ly	=	likely
same	+	ness	=	sameness

Exceptions

argue	+	ment	=	argument
canoe	+	ing	=	canoeing
change	+	able	=	changeable
courage	+	ous	=	courageous
judge	+	ment	=	judgment
manage	+	able	=	manageable
mile	+	age	=	mileage
notice	+	able	=	noticeable
true	+	ly	=	truly

DOCUMENTATION GUIDE

1 DIFFERENT STYLES OF DOCUMENTATION

To ensure uniformity and to simplify the reader's task, each academic discipline has its own strict rules for documentation. These rules dictate the ways in which quoted, paraphrased, or summarized material is acknowledged in notes and in bibliographies. For information on the particulars of manuscript preparation and parenthetical and bibliographic citations, consult the appropriate references from the following list:

Biology
- *CBE Style Manual: A Guide for Authors, Editors, and Publishers in the Biological Sciences.* 5th ed. Bethesda, MD: Council of Biology Editors, 1983.

Chemistry
- *Handbook for Authors of Papers in American Chemical Society Publications.* Washington, D.C.: American Chemical Society, 1978.

Geology
- *Geowriting: A Guide to Writing, Editing, and Printing in Earth Science.* Alexandria, VA: American Geological Institute, 1984.

Humanities, Language, and Literature
- *MLA Handbook for Writers of Research Papers.* 3rd ed. New York: Modern Language Association of America, 1988.

Law
- *A Uniform System of Citation.* 14th ed. Cambridge, MA: Harvard Law Review, 1986.

Linguistics
- "LSA Style Sheet." Appears annually in the *LSA Bulletin,* December issue.

Mathematics
- *A Manual for Authors of Mathematical Papers.* 7th ed. Providence, RI: American Mathematical Society, 1980.

DOCUMENTATION GUIDE

Medicine
- "Uniform Requirements for Manuscripts Submitted to Biomedical Journals." *Annals of Internal Medicine* 90. 1(1979). [International Steering Committee of Medical Editors.]

Physics
- *Style Manual for Guidance in the Preparation of Papers.* 3rd ed. New York: American Institute of Physics, 1978.

Social Sciences
- *Publication Manual of the American Psychological Association.* 3rd ed. Washington, DC: American Psychological Association, 1983.

In the humanities (literature, language studies, art history, music appreciation, theater, film studies, and foreign languages), the style of the Modern Language Association (MLA) is most often used. Always consult your instructor before choosing a style guide.

2 MLA STYLE OF DOCUMENTATION

Scholars and researchers alike use a two- or three-tiered system of documenting borrowed information, whether that information is summarized, paraphrased, or quoted directly. Paying strict attention to this system will make you a more credible writer and prevent inadvertent plagiarism.

Level One (works cited list)

Writers following the guidelines of the MLA system of documentation call the list of sources for a paper *Works Cited*. Writers and researchers should be able to use this bibliographic record to re-create or expand on your research. The Works Cited list appears at the end of your research paper. Each entry contains information regarding authorship; title of text, article, or other work; place and date of publication; and related matters.

Level Two (parenthetical citations)

To acknowledge your debt to other authors properly, you should attribute material to sources and incorporate references within the body of your writing. The usual method for doing this is often called *parenthetical citation*. Your aim is to offer the reader enough information within the text to identify a particular entry in the Works Cited list and to specify the exact page location of the original material.

Unlike MLA, some style guides and some instructors require that the information about sources be placed at the end of the paper (as endnotes) or at the bottom of the page (as footnotes). A superscript (raised number) in the text alerts the reader to the citation.

If possible, introduce quoted material by acknowledging the author or both the author and source in your sentence. This makes referencing easier and adds authority to your own work:

DOCUMENTATION GUIDE

>According to Martin Pawley, writing in his landmark book, Building for Tomorrow: Putting Garbage to Work, recycling's "chief drawback is that the energy that went into giving the bottle its distinctive shape or the can its remarkable dimensional shape is lost" (109).

If the quotation won't fit into your sentence easily, you may opt to acknowledge the source at the end of the borrowed material instead:

>"Today most of the design work in resource recovery is going to the development of doomsday machines capable of crushing and burying everything that we make," comments Pawley (151).

Acknowledgment of the author can also be made with such expressions as *according to, states that, in the words of, remarks that, points out that, says that, claims that,* and *concludes by saying that.*

If your Works Cited section contains more than one work by a single author, you'll have to give an abbreviated form of the title along with the page number, as follows:

>According to Fenton, no mention is made of the plastic recovery process known as "reintegration" before 1990 (Remanufacturing 343).

If the author's name is not introduced within the text, it should appear in parentheses with the page number.

>According to the author, "The remanufactured machines reportedly met or exceeded corporate expectations of uptime, utilization, and networkability" (Kirkland 45).

Level Three (explanatory notes)

Writers occasionally need to include explanatory footnotes at the bottom of the page or at the end of the paper. These notes

MLA STYLE OF DOCUMENTATION D-5

may point readers to sources not listed in the Works Cited list or explain concepts, terms, or references essential to an understanding of the work. Some writers also use explanatory notes to go into detail about interesting but peripheral points. If you decide to use explanatory footnotes in a paper, use the superscript system:

In the text: Tupperware engineers redesign their molding machinery on the basis of feedback they receive from workers who use the machinery.[2]

At bottom of page (or end of paper): [2]Although the Tupperware company has not published a study of its machine conversions or remanufacturing processes, this information is available to interested parties through Tupperware's public relations department.

MLA Works Cited

The Works Cited list provides readers with essential information that allows them to make sense of your research process. At minimum, an MLA Works Cited entry contains the following information:

- Names of all authors or editors
- Title of the work
- Place of publication, publisher, and date of publication
- Page numbers (for articles and works in collections)

The directory on page D-6 will help you find most of the formats you'll need to set up the Works Cited list for a typical research paper in the MLA style.

The following guide explains and gives an example for each type of work.

DOCUMENTATION GUIDE

MLA FORMAT DIRECTORY

Books
Book by a single author, D-6
More than one work by the same author, D-7
Two or three authors or editors, D-7
More than three authors or editors, D-7
Corporate or group author, D-7
Single editor, D-7
Translation, D-8
Republished book, D-8
Edition other than the first, D-8
Work in two or more volumes, D-8
Work in an anthology, D-8
Unpublished dissertation, D-9

Periodicals
Article in a weekly or twice-monthly magazine, D-9
Article in a monthly or bimonthly magazine, D-9
Article in a journal paginated continuously by volume, D-9
Article in a journal paginated separately by issue, D-10
Unsigned article in a periodical, D-10
Book review in a periodical, D-10
Signed article in a newspaper, D-10
Letter to an editor, D-11

Other Sources
Lecture, D-11
Interview, D-11
Dictionary entry, D-11
Encyclopedia entry, D-11
Audio recording, D-11
Computer software, D-12
Videotape or film, D-12
Television or radio program, D-12
Government publication, D-12

Books (MLA format)

Single author. Invert author's name. Underline the complete title. Give both the city and state or country of the publisher when the city alone might not be clear. Obtain publication information from the title page of the book or the copyright page that follows. If more than one city is given, use the first; if more than one date, use the most recent. Use a shortened version of the publisher's name. Abbreviate *University Press* as *UP*. Note that when an entry is more than one line long, subsequent lines should be indented *five spaces*.

Piccione, Anthony. <u>Seeing It Was So</u>. Brockport, NY:
    BOA Editions, 1986.

More than one work by the same author. When citing two or more books written by the same author, indicate the author's name only in the first entry; thereafter, use three hyphens followed by a period in place of the name. List works by the same author alphabetically by title.

Everwine, Peter. <u>Collecting the Animals</u>. New York:
    Atheneum, 1976.
- - -. <u>Keeping the Night</u>. New York: Atheneum, 1977.

Two or three authors or editors. Invert only the name of the first author. Give names as they appear on the book's title page.

Knoblauch, C. H., and Lil Brannon. <u>Rhetorical Traditions and the Teaching of Writing</u>. Upper Montclair, NJ: Boynton/Cook, 1984.

More than three authors or editors. Use the abbreviation *et al.* ("and others") after the initial author.

Belanoff, Pat, et al. <u>The Right Handbook</u>. Upper
    Montclair, NJ: Boynton/Cook, 1986.

Corporate or group author. Use the corporate author as both the author and publisher, if necessary.

Environmental Defense Fund. <u>Secondary Containment:
    A Second Line of Defense</u>. New York: Environmental Defense Fund, 1985.

Single editor. Use the single-author format, add a comma and the abbreviation *ed.*

D-8 DOCUMENTATION GUIDE

>Franzosa, Bob, ed. Grateful Dead Folktales. Orono, ME: Zosafarm Publ., 1989.

Translation. Highlight either the original writer or the translator, depending on the focus of your paper. (*UP* is the MLA abbreviation for *University Press*.)

>Botwinik, Berl. Lead Pencil: Stories and Sketches by Berl Botwinik. Trans. Philip J. Klukoff. Detroit: Wayne State UP, 1984.

Republished book. Add the date of the original publication after the title. End the citation with the current publication date.

>Polyani, Michael. Personal Knowledge: Towards a Post-Critical Philosophy. 1958. Chicago: U of Chicago P, 1962.

Edition other than the first. Place the edition number and *ed.* after the full title.

>Ruggiero, Vincent Ryan. The Art of Thinking: A Guide to Critical and Creative Thought. 3rd ed. New York: Harper, 1991.

Work in two or more volumes. Include the total number of volumes, whether you use more than one or not. Insert the volume information before the publication reference.

>Bonfantamantin, Reginald. The Jewish Mystique. 3 vols. New York: Achshav, 1977.

Work in an anthology. Highlight the author of the selection, rather than the editor of the anthology. The editor's name follows the title of the anthology, preceded by the abbreviation

Ed. Give the page numbers of the entire work, not just those pages you have cited.

> Bettelheim, Bruno. "The Informed Heart." <u>Out of the Whirlwind: A Reader of Holocaust Literature.</u> Ed. Albert Friedlander. New York: Schocken, 1976 48-63.

Unpublished dissertation. Take care to put the dissertation title in quotation marks, followed by the abbreviation *Diss.*

> Wilensky, Harold L. "The Staff 'Expert': A Study of the Intelligence Functions in American Trade Unions." Diss. U of Chicago, 1953.

Periodicals (MLA format)

Article in a weekly or twice-monthly magazine. Give the periodical's complete date, in inverted abbreviated form, followed by a colon and the page range for the entire article.

> Corliss, Richard. "Do Stars Deliver?" <u>Time</u> 26 Aug. 1991: 38-40.

Article in a monthly or bimonthly magazine. Give the month and year. Use a hyphen between months for a bimonthly publication.

> Murphy, Bob. "Modern Neo-Pagans." <u>Utne Reader</u> Nov.-Dec. 1991: 22-26.

Article in a journal paginated continuously by volume. In a periodical with continuous pagination, if the first issue for a year ends on page 216, the second issue will begin with page 217. In such a periodical, give the volume number, the year in parentheses, and the page numbers of the entire article, not just those you have cited.

Coles, Robert. "Public Evil and Private Problems:
    Segregation and Psychiatry." Yale Review 54
    (1965): 513-31.

Article in a journal paginated separately by issue. For a periodical that begins each issue with page 1, give the volume number and the issue number, separated by a period.

Revell, Donald. "'Abesces': The Oz and Sheol of
    James Tate." Willow Springs 25.2 (1990): 63-89.

Unsigned article in a periodical. For anonymous articles, use the title in the author slot, and alphabetize the entry by its title.

"Dough Conditioners: Pizzeria Question Mark."
    Pizza World Jan. 1990: 23-24.

Book review in a periodical. Give author and title of review, followed by *Rev. of* and the title of the work reviewed. (Do not underline, italicize, or place inside quotation marks the words *Rev. of.*) Follow the title of the work with *by* and the name of the work's author. Include the name of the publication and appropriate publication information. If the name of the reviewer is not known, begin with the title of the review.

Smith, Raymond J. "Some Poetic Self-Revelations."
    Rev. of American Poets in 1976, ed. William
    Heyen. Ontario Review 5 (1976-77): 102-04.

Signed article in a newspaper. Include the author's name, the title of the article, the date and edition, and the section and page numbers if applicable. If the article is unsigned, leave the title of the article in the position usually occupied by the author's name and alphabetize by title.

Sullivan, Barbara. "Burning Ambition." Chicago Tribune 21 May 1992, late ed., sec. 7: 11.

Letter to an editor. Include the word *Letter* after the author's name.

```
Lovis, Adrian C. Letter. AWP Chronicle 24.1 (1991):
    17-18.
```

Other sources (MLA format)

Lecture. Use a description unless an organization, meeting, or title is available.

```
Anderson, Mary Victoria. Class lecture, English 095.
    Loyola U of Chicago. 21 Oct. 1991.
```

Interview. If the interview is conducted by the researcher, indicate the name and date of the person interviewed and include a descriptive phrase such as *Personal interview.*

```
Avrahami, Nir, and Ilene Greenberg. Personal inter-
    view. 6 July 1988.
```

Dictionary entry. Follow the rules for a work in an anthology.

```
"Experimental Design." Modern Dictionary of Sociol-
    ogy. Ed. George A. Theodorson and Achilles G.
    Theodorson. New York: Crowell, 1969.
```

Encyclopedia entry. Follow the rules for a work in an anthology. If articles are arranged alphabetically, you may omit volume and page numbers.

```
Fussell, Paul. "Meter." Encyclopedia of Poetry and
    Poetics. Ed. Alex Preminger. Princeton, NJ:
    Princeton UP, 1965.
```

Audio recording. Your purpose will determine whether you highlight performer, conductor, composer, or title. Give catalog number, if possible.

DOCUMENTATION GUIDE

> Garcia, Jerry. Jerry Garcia Band. With John Kahn,
> Melvin Seals, David Kemper, Jackie La Branch,
> and Gloria James. Arista, 07822-18690-2, 1991.

Computer software. In the case of company authorship, indicate company name. Include as much description as possible: system, size, medium.

> Sweitzer, Keith. Backup Master: High Performance Hard
> Disk Backup Utility. Computer software. Inter-
> secting Concepts, 1986. IBM, 160kb, 5.25" disk.

Videotape or film. Include title, director, and other significant participants (such as writers or performers).

> Teenage Mutant Ninja Turtles: The Shredder Is Splin-
> tered. Based on characters and comic books cre-
> ated by Kevin Eastman and Peter Laird. Mirage
> Studios, 1988.

Television or radio program. Generally, place the episode title in quotations first, followed by writer, title of program, other contributors, network, local station and city, and the date of broadcast.

> "Youth." Writ. Roseanne Arnold. Roseanne. Prod.
> Marcy Carsey and Tom Werner. With John Good-
> man. WABC, New York. 29 Oct. 1991.

Government publication. If no author is given, list the government first, followed by the actual agency. Cite the printer in the publisher slot (in the United States, usually *GPO*, the U.S. Government Printing Office).

> United States. Environmental Protection Agency.
> Chemicals in Your Community: A Guide to the

<u>Emergency Planning and Community Right-to-Know</u>
<u>Act</u>. Washington, DC: GPO, 1988.

When following the MLA style of manuscript preparation and documentation, keep these basic considerations in mind:

MLA STYLE OF MANUSCRIPT PREPARATION

- Type or print clearly on white paper. Check with your instructor before submitting copy prepared on a dot-matrix printer.
- For your protection, always keep a copy of the original.
- As a rule, double-space your text (including the Works Cited list and any notes). Indent five space to indicate the beginning of a paragraph. Indent ten spaces from the left margin to show a set-off quotation.
- Allow for one-inch margins at the top, bottom, and on both sides of your paper (page numbers appear at the right margin, half an inch below the top of the page).
- Provide a title page and report cover if you want to or if your instructor requires them. Otherwise, include all relevant information on the first page. Do not number the title page.
- Indicate your last name and page number of *all* pages beginning with the first (including notes, Works Cited list, and appendixes).

Always check with your instructors regarding their preferences for manuscript formatting and presentation.

3 APA STYLE OF DOCUMENTATION

Parenthetical citations

Researchers following the system devised by the American Psychological Association (APA) link their parenthetical citations to a References section. In the APA system, the page number or range appears in parentheses at the end of a quotation, preceded by the abbreviation *p.* or *pp.* The author's name usually appears at the beginning of the sentence, the publication date, in parentheses, follows it immediately:

```
According to Kirkland (1991), "The remanufactured ma-
chines reportedly met or exceeded corporate expectations
of uptime, utilization, and networkability" (p. 45).
```

If the author's name does not appear in the sentence, it is given in parentheses with the year and the page number, separated by commas:

```
According to the author, "The remanufactured
machines reportedly met or exceeded corporate
expectations of uptime, utilization, and networkability"
(Kirkland, 1991, p. 45).
```

In a summary or paraphrase, the page number is optional, but the author's name and the date of publication must be included.

```
Miller (1981) describes patients who were not
allowed to express their feelings as children because
they had had a narcissistic parent.

Patients were not allowed to express their feelings
as children because they had had a narcissistic parent
(Miller, 1981).
```

APA FORMAT DIRECTORY

Books
Single author, D-16
More than one work by the same author, D-16
Two or more authors or editors, D-16
Corporate or group author, D-16
Edited book, D-17
Work in an anthology, D-17
Translation, D-17
Edition other than the first, D-17
Unpublished dissertation or manuscript, D-17

Periodicals
Article in a weekly or twice-monthly magazine, D-18
Article in a journal paginated continuously by volume, D-18
Article in a journal paginated separately by issue, D-18
Book review in a periodical, D-18
Article in a newspaper, D-19
Unsigned newspaper article, D-19
Letter to an editor, D-19

Other Sources
Published interview, D-19
Government document, D-19
Audio recording, D-20
Videotape or film, D-20
Computer software, D-20

If a work has more than one author, both authors should be named in the text. Use an ampersand (&) if the names are given in parentheses: (Thompson & Hickey, 1994, p. 48).

APA references

The basic APA references entry contains the following information:

- Names of all authors or editors
- Title of the work
- Place of publication, publisher, and date of publication
- Page numbers (articles and works in collections)

DOCUMENTATION GUIDE

The directory on page D-15 will help you locate most of the formats you'll need to set up the References section for a typical research paper done in APA style.

The following guide explains and gives an example for each type of reference.

Books (APA format)

Single author. Invert author's name, and reduce all given names to initials. Give year of publication next, in parentheses. Capitalize only the first word and proper nouns in the title (and the first word following the colon in a subtitle). When an entry is more than one line long, subsequent lines indent *three spaces*.

> Kroeber, T. (1961). Ishi in two worlds: A biography of the last wild Indians in North America. Berkeley: University of California Press.

More than one work by the same author. Use author's name for each work. List in chronological order.

> Cassirer, E. (1944). An essay on man. New Haven, CT: Yale University Press.
>
> Cassirer, E. (1961). The logic of the humanities. New Haven, CT: Yale University Press.

Two or more authors or editors. Provide the names of all authors, inverted. Use an ampersand (&) before the last.

> Kinsey, A. C., Pomeroy, W. B., & Martin, C. E. (1948). Sexual behavior in the human male. Philadelphia: Saunders.

Corporate or group author. When the author and publisher are the same, use *Author* in the publisher slot.

Environmental Defense Fund. (1988). <u>Coming full
circle: Successful recycling today</u>. New York: Author.

Edited book. After the name or names, insert *(Ed.)* or *(Eds.)*.

Cumming, R. D. (Ed.). (1965). <u>The philosophy of
Jean-Paul Sartre</u>. New York: Random House.

Work in an anthology. Cite the author of the work, not of the anthology. Use no quotation marks. Give page numbers of the entire article.

Bettelheim, B. (1980). Eichmann: The systems, the
victims. In B. Bettelheim (Ed.), <u>Surviving</u> (pp.
258-273). New York: Vintage.

Translation. Show the original author and title, followed by the translator.

Neumann, E. (1973). <u>Depth psychology and a new
ethic</u> (E. Rolfe, Trans.). New York: Harper.
(Original work published 1949)

Edition other than the first. Abbreviate edition *ed.* in parentheses after the title.

Evans-Wentz, W. Y. (Ed.). (1960). <u>The Tibetan book
of the dead</u> (3rd ed.). London: Oxford University Press.

Unpublished dissertation or manuscript. Describe the manuscript appropriately *(M.A. thesis, Ph.D. dissertation,* and so on).

Rosenbaum, G. (1953). An analysis of personalization in neighborhood apparel retailing. Unpublished M.A. thesis, Department of Sociology, University of Chicago.

Periodicals (APA format)

Article in a weekly or twice-monthly magazine. Include issue date in parentheses after author's name. Page numbers (of the entire article) appear last.

Strykeer, P. (1953, August). How executives get jobs. Fortune, pp. 182-194.

Article in a journal paginated continuously by volume. In a journal with continuous pagination, if the first issue of a volume ends on page 302, the next issue will begin on page 303. For such a journal, provide only the volume number (underscored) and pages; do not give issue information.

Winnicott, D. W. (1969). The use of an object. International Journal of Psychoanalysis, 50, 700-716.

Article in a journal paginated separately by issue. For a journal that begins each issue on page 1, give volume number, issue number in parentheses, and page references.

Hart, H. (1989). Seamus Heaney's anxiety of trust in field work. Chicago Review, 36(3), 87-108.

Book review in a periodical. Bracket *Review of* and the title of the book being reviewed. Complete periodical format.

Homes, R. J. (1991, September). [Review of A reference guide to media bias]. Bloomsbury Review, p. 7.

Article in a newspaper. Cite full date in parentheses after author's name.

>   Mateja, J. (1991, October 27). Chrysler planning a
>   battery-powered mini-van. Chicago Tribune,
>   pp. T3, T8.

Unsigned newspaper article. Provide the title of the article in first position; then follow newspaper article format.

>   Reader's guide to the silver screen. (1991, October
>   25). Chicago Reader, pp. 33-36.

Letter to an editor. If the letter as published has no heading, use the first sentence as title. Bracket the description *Letter to the editor*.

>   Smith, L. (1991, September). DAT deterioration?
>   [Letter to the editor]. Stereo Review, p. 9.

Other sources (APA format)

Published interview. Bracket *Interview with* and the person's name. (APA does not reference unpublished interviews.)

>   Auer, T. (1991, July-August). Montana memories
>   [Interview with Ivan Doig]. Bloomsbury Review,
>   pp. 9-20.

Government document. Style as for a book with one author.

>   Environmental Protection Agency. (1988). Medical
>   waste: EPA environmental backgrounder. Washing-
>   ton, DC: EPA, Office of Public Affairs.

DOCUMENTATION GUIDE

Audio recording. Provide catalog number, if available.

Youman, B. (Producer), & Rivers, B. (Narrator). (1991). TDK's ultimate guide to recording from CDs [Compact Disc Recording CDK 0100]. Port Washington, NY: TDK Electronics.

Videotape or film. Use the name of producer, director, or writer as author, depending on your focus. Bracket the description *Videotape*.

Smith, G. W. (Producer). (1988). Your water, your life [Videotape]. Washington, DC: Public Interest Video Network.

Computer software. Indicate writer or group, followed by release numbers. Bracket description *Computer program*.

WordStar International. (1989). WordStar Release 5.5 [Computer program]. San Rafael, CA: WordStar International.

4 CBE STYLE OF DOCUMENTATION

If you are writing a paper for a course in the natural sciences, one accepted guide for documentation and manuscript preparation is the *CBE Style Manual,* published by the Council of Biology Editors. CBE style includes two methods of documentation, one similar to APA style and another system that uses numbers. In the numbered system, sources are listed on the References page either in alphabetical order or in the order in which they are cited. Each reference has a number, and this number is given in parentheses in the text when a source is cited.

```
Thomas (1) maintains that our national fixation on
health is a symptom of our fear of dying.
```

In the References list, the entry for that source, the basic entry for a book with one author, would look like this:

```
1. Thomas, L. The Medusa and the snail. New
   York: Penguin; 1981.
```

Capitalize only the first word in the title and any proper nouns. Do not underline or italicize the title. Use a semicolon to separate the date from the publisher. If the note is more than one line long, subsequent lines should begin under the first letter of the author's last name.

Other CBE entries

Book with two or more authors. Use semicolons to separate all authors' names, regardless of number.

```
2. Minnich, J.; Hunt, M. The Rodale guide to com-
   posting. Emmaus, PA: Rodale Press; 1979.
```

Book with a corporate or group author. Place the corporation or group name in the author slot.

   3. Natural Resources Defense Council. Cooling the greenhouse: vital first steps to combat global warming. Washington, DC: Government Printing Office; 1988.

Book with a single editor. Spell out the word *editor*; otherwise follow the rules for a book with a single author.

   4. Busnel, R. G., editor. Acoustic behavior of animals. Amsterdam: Elsevier; 1963.

Work in an anthology. List the author of the work first, then the title followed by *In:*, and then the author or editor of the anthology, the title of the anthology, and publication information.

   5. Wilson, E. O. Chemical systems. In: Seboek, T. A., editor. Animal communication: techniques of study and results of research. Bloomington: Indiana University Press; 1970: 200-221.

Article in journal paginated continuously by volume. In a journal with continuous pagination, if the first issue of a volume ends on page 228, the next issue will begin on page 229. A colon (but no space) is used between volume and page numbers.

   6. Wiener, H. External chemical messengers. New York State Journal of Medicine 66:3153-3170; 1968.

Magazine article. Only the first word and any proper nouns are capitalized in the title of the article.

7. Bettelheim, B. Surviving. <u>New Yorker</u>. 1976 August 2:31-52.